MAKING FRIENDS FOR GOD

Other books by Mark Finley

10 Days in the Upper Room

The Church Triumphant

End-Time Living

Fulfilling God's End-Time Mission

Hope Beyond Tomorrow

Revive Us Again

Studying Together: A Ready-Reference Bible Handbook

What the Bible Says About

When God Said Remember

MAKING FRIENDS FOR GOD
Mark Finley

Pacific Press®
Publishing Association
Nampa, Idaho | www.pacificpress.com

Cover design and resources from Lars Justinen

Copyright © 2020 by Pacific Press® Publishing Association
Printed in the United States of America
All rights reserved

Additional copies of this book are available for purchase by calling toll-free 1-800-765-6955 or by visiting AdventistBookCenter.com.

Library of Congress Cataloging-in-Publication Data

Names: Finley, Mark, 1945- author.
Title: Making friends for God / Mark Finley.
Description: Nampa, Idaho : Pacific Press Publishing Association, 2020. | Includes
    bibliographical references. | Summary: "This book is about soul-winning principles
    involved with sharing Christ's love and truth. Witnessing is the role of each believer
    and comes as the natural result of knowing Jesus. Following in His footsteps, one can
    discover the universal principles for sharing their faith"— Provided by publisher.
Identifiers: LCCN 2019049458 | ISBN 9780816365876 (paperback) |
    ISBN 9780816365883 (ebook)
Subjects: LCSH: Witness bearing (Christianity)
Classification: LCC BV4520 .F525 2020 | DDC 248/.5—dc23
LC record available at https://lccn.loc.gov/2019049458

February 2020

Contents

Introduction

Sometimes I am asked, "How long does it take you to write a book?" Of course, that depends on a variety of factors, such as the topic, the length of the book, and the research necessary to bolster the facts. It also depends on the target audience—the people who will read the book. This book is different. It took me fifty-three years to write. That's right; it's not a typographical error—fifty-three years.

This book is different from many of the more than seventy books I have already written. In it, I will share the soul-winning principles I have discovered over more than half of a century of sharing Christ's love and truth in countries around the world. Over the decades, I have learned that witnessing is not complicated, and it is certainly not the role of a few supersmart spiritual giants. Neither is witnessing one of the spiritual gifts listed in Scripture.

Witnessing is the role of each believer. When we come to Christ and are changed by His grace, charmed by His love, and redeemed by His power, we cannot be silent. We long to tell the story of the living Christ with others. Our hearts burn within us to share what Jesus has done for us. Witnessing is the natural result of knowing Jesus. So join me on this journey as we travel in the footsteps of Jesus and discover the universal principles of sharing our faith.

One

Why Witness?

Deep in God's heart is a desire for all people to be saved in His kingdom. He longs for each of His children to experience the joy of salvation and eternal life. He has unleashed all the powers of heaven to redeem us. Without you, there would be an empty space in heaven, and that is why nothing is more important to the Father, Son, and Holy Spirit than your salvation.

The apostle Paul makes this clear when he declares, "For this is good and acceptable in the sight of God our Savior, who desires all men to be saved and come to the knowledge of the truth" (1 Timothy 2:3, 4). Do you grasp the significance of this statement? God has an intense longing, a deep desire, an overriding purpose in all He does. He wants you and me to be saved and live in the light of His truth. The apostle Peter states that God is "not willing that any should perish" (2 Peter 3:9). The salvation of man is heaven's priority. Jesus Christ, the eternal, coexistent, all-wise, all-powerful Son of God, is our Advocate. At His bidding, angels wing their way from the heavenly courts to beat back the demonic forces that wage battle against us. Daily, the Holy Spirit impresses our minds and guides our lives.

To accomplish our salvation, Jesus came to earth, revealing the Father's measureless love for humanity. He lived the perfect life we should have lived, bore the condemnation of our sins, and died the death we should have died. In Christ, we see the character of the Father. Jesus dispels the myth that God is unloving. Long ago, Lucifer, a being of dazzling brightness, misrepresented God's character. His lies distorted the image of God before the entire universe (John 8:44). Jesus came to set the record straight, proving that God is not a vindictive judge or a wrathful tyrant. He is a loving Father who wants to gather all His children home.

The heart of all witnessing

Telling the story of redemption is the task of witnessing. It begins with a declaration of God's faithfulness and ends with the triumph of His love. Through believers, God reaches His lost children. In our lives and speech, people see His gracious character. Our witness to others becomes life's greatest joy. As we grow to be more like Jesus, service comes naturally, and selfishness is starved to death. The more we share His love, the more our love for Him grows.

But many raise fair questions about witnessing. Isn't God doing everything He can to save people without my witness? Why should I share my faith? Does witnessing make any difference at all in an individual's salvation?

In answer to the first question, it is true that God is not limited to the witness of human beings. He has revealed Himself in a variety of ways. David notes the wonders of creation:

The heavens declare the glory of God;
And the firmament shows His handiwork.
Day unto day utters speech,
And night unto night reveals knowledge.
There is no speech or language
Where their voice is not heard (Psalm 19:1, 2).

The design, order, and symmetry of the universe reveal a designer God of infinite intelligence.

Additionally, the ministry of the Holy Spirit in our hearts

creates a desire to know God. This longing for eternity within is convincing evidence of the existence of God (Ecclesiastes 3:11). And, of course, there are special providences that cause us to reflect on the reality of God's presence. Each time we experience undeserved love or an unexpected kindness, we witness a revelation of God's character. He is persuasive, seeking to draw us to Himself.

If this is true, then why witness? Why not let God do His job and be done with it? The challenge of relying on nature as a witness involves the problem of sin. Marred by evil, nature often delivers mixed messages. Although it reveals God's design, it also reveals destruction and devastation. Hurricanes, floods, forest fires, typhoons, and other natural disasters plague our planet. Thousands die suddenly. What do these tragedies say about God and the great controversy between good and evil? This question undoubtedly complicates nature's witness. Beauty and destruction lie close together. The natural world includes both aspects of our reality, yet it stops short of revealing the reason why good and evil coexist.

Nature and our life experience send mixed messages about the goodness of God. Herein lies the reason for our witness. The story of Jesus, as told in Scripture, reconciles the incongruities of nature and our internal struggles. Though nature and the providences of life render evidence of God's existence, they do not clearly portray His loving character. Their witness is incomplete. God has always understood this void and carefully planned that the clearest revelation of His character would be found in the life of Christ, as revealed in the Bible. When we share the truth about Jesus with others, we offer them the best chance of knowing and understanding God's love for them. In the cosmic conflict between good and evil, Scripture presents the ultimate answers to life's most important questions.

In addition to this fundamental truth about witnessing, we tell the story because we know that witnessing is one of Heaven's means of bringing joy to the heart of God and enabling us to grow spiritually. The more we love Him, the more we will share His love, and the more we share His love, the more we will love

Him. As we share the Word of God with others, we are drawn closer to Him. The life-changing Word not only changes those with whom we study the Bible but also changes us.

There is a powerful passage in *Steps to Christ* that discusses the relationship between witnessing and our personal spiritual growth:

If you will go to work as Christ designs that His disciples shall, and win souls for Him, you will feel the need of a deeper experience and a greater knowledge in divine things, and will hunger and thirst after righteousness. You will plead with God, and your faith will be strengthened, and your soul will drink deeper drafts at the well of salvation. Encountering opposition and trials will drive you to the Bible and prayer. You will grow in grace and the knowledge of Christ, and will develop a rich experience.

The spirit of unselfish labor for others gives depth, stability, and Christlike loveliness to the character, and brings peace and happiness to its possessor. The aspirations are elevated. There is no room for sloth or selfishness. Those who thus exercise the Christian graces will grow and will become strong to work for God. They will have clear spiritual perceptions, a steady, growing faith, and an increased power in prayer. The Spirit of God, moving upon their spirit, calls forth the sacred harmonies of the soul in answer to the divine touch. Those who thus devote themselves to unselfish effort for the good of others are most surely working out their own salvation.

The only way to grow in grace is to be disinterestedly doing the very work which Christ has enjoined upon us—to engage, to the extent of our ability, in helping and blessing those who need the help we can give them. Strength comes by exercise; activity is the very condition of life.[1]

Why Witness?

This insightful passage offers four lessons on soul winning:

1. Soul winning leads us to feel the need for a more profound spiritual experience.
2. Soul winning leads us to plead with God until our faith is strengthened.
3. Soul winning gives us depth, stability, and Christlike loveliness.
4. Soul winning gives us clear spiritual perceptions; a steady, growing faith; and an increased power in prayer.

In addition to drawing us closer to God, the blessing of witnessing is twofold: it provides a way for others to be saved, and it nourishes our languishing souls.

Witnessing and God's heart

The motivation for witnessing comes from appreciating God's passion for saving the lost. No Bible chapter illustrates this better than Luke 15. Here the Gospel writer sweeps aside the curtain on God's heart and reveals three pictures of His love. He is the tireless shepherd who seeks the lost sheep until He finds it. He is the sorrowful woman who, on her knees, searches for the precious lost coin from her wedding dowry. He is the anxious father, scanning the horizon for the return of his lost son. In each story, when the lost are found, there is tremendous joy. All of heaven rejoices when men and women accept the salvation that Christ purchased at Calvary.

In the first story, the story of the lost sheep, Jesus teaches three significant lessons. First, God's love pursues the lost. Luke 15:4 declares that the shepherd goes after the lost sheep. Our God is a pursuing God. He will not let His children go easily. He seeks them wherever they may wander. With relentless love, He searches for them. Second, we notice that the shepherd goes after the sheep until he finds it. God's love perseveres. He does not give up on us easily. We cannot weary Him. He will never abandon His search. In Christ's time, if a Middle Eastern shepherd lost one of his sheep, it was expected that he would return to the flock with the lost sheep or return to the flock with the carcass of the lost sheep. He had to demonstrate that he had done everything possible to find it. Each sheep was valuable to the shepherd. He knew the flock so well that he was immediately aware when a sheep was missing. To Christ, we are not a mass of nameless humanity; we are individuals created in His image and redeemed by His grace.

Finally, when the lost sheep is found, the shepherd celebrates. "Rejoice with me, for I have found my sheep which was lost!" (verse 6). The Good Shepherd does not rest until He finds His lost sheep, and when it is found, there is tremendous joy. This joy theme is consistent in all the Luke 15 parables. When the coin is found, the woman exclaims with joy, "Rejoice with me, for I have found the piece which I lost!" (verse 9). When the prodigal son returns, his father shouts for joy and throws a party (verses 22–24). Each of these parables dramatically concludes with the joy of finding the lost. Though many things sadden God and bring tears to His eyes, His heart is filled with joy when we participate in soul winning. When we join Him in His single-minded quest to find the lost, His heart is filled with unspeakable joy.

Have you ever spent hours searching for just the right gift? Maybe it's a birthday, anniversary, or Christmas present you're seeking. When you finally find the perfect gift, you are thrilled. It matches both the person and the event. You can hardly wait to share it. With great anticipation, the day arrives, the gift is unwrapped, and that special someone is delighted. Unprompted, they throw their arms around you and say, "Thank you so much!"

Who received greater joy from the gift? you, or the one who received it? Of course, both of you were elated, but there is an exceptional satisfaction that comes with giving something of value to someone else. Unselfish gift giving creates a strong and unique bond between people.

When we share the most precious gift of all, Jesus Christ, pure joy fills our hearts. There is deep satisfaction in knowing we have made an eternal difference in someone's life. Ellen

White describes the experience in *Steps to Christ*:

> The humblest and poorest of the disciples of Jesus can be a blessing to others. They may not realize that they are doing any special good, but by their unconscious influence they may start waves of blessing that will widen and deepen, and the blessed results they may never know until the day of final reward. They do not feel or know that they are doing anything great. They are not required to weary themselves with anxiety about success. They have only to go forward quietly, doing faithfully the work that God's providence assigns, and their life will not be in vain. Their own souls will be growing more and more into the likeness of Christ; they are workers together with God in this life and are thus fitting for the higher work and the unshadowed joy of the life to come.[2]

It is still an eternal truth that "it is more blessed to give than to receive" (Acts 20:35).

Your circle of influence

Think of someone in your sphere of influence who might be receptive to knowing more about Jesus. A son or a daughter, maybe a husband or a wife, a work colleague, neighbor, or friend. Picture the person's face and ask God to create an opportunity for you to guide the conversation in a spiritual direction. Do not feel you have to create an opportunity that does not present itself. The mission is God's. We do not create opportunities; He does. Our role is to be sensitive to the opportunities and cooperate with Him by walking through the doors He opens.

A story I heard recently illustrates the value of taking a particular interest in someone. Dr. Marilyn Hellenberg taught English at Kearney State College. One semester, she had a student named Kwan. On the opening day of class, she asked the students to write a simple statement about themselves. Kwan wrote: "I think English is a real bore. My main hobby is harassing stupid teachers, and English teachers are the stupidest of all."

Kwan was disruptive throughout the entire class period. He had a callous disregard for the feelings of other students. As Dr. Hellenberg prayed that night, she was deeply impressed to see Kwan through God's eyes. He was created by God, valued by God, and loved by God. She prayed that she would be able to see Kwan as Christ saw him.

As the semester progressed, Dr. Hellenberg tried every way possible to make Kwan feel accepted in class. But her efforts were to no avail. He continued his belligerent, disruptive ways.

One day, before reading a poem, she announced to the class, "Kwan, this poem is dedicated to you." The poem was "Outwitted," written by Edwin Markham.

He drew a circle and shut me out—
Heretic, rebel, a thing to flout.
But Love and I had the wit to win:
We drew a circle that took him in!

After class one day, Kwan lingered to ask a question: "Why don't you just give up on me?" Before Dr. Hellenberg could reply, he went on to confide, "You can't let people get too close to you. I play a game in which I try to hurt them before they hurt me. I have been rejected so many times; I cannot take it any longer."

In his final essay, Kwan wrote, "There are three kinds of teachers. Those who are interesting but stupid, those who are intelligent but boring, and those who are both boring and stupid like my English teacher."

When Dr. Hellenberg read his final paper in the quietness of her office, she burst into tears. "Lord, I have tried to reach this boy, and I cannot take it any longer. My efforts have been in vain. I have invested so much emotional energy in him; I am drained."

After returning his final essay to him, she added one final thought, "Kwan, I can't play mind games with you. I care for you because God created you. You are His child." Without further elaboration, she turned, walked back to her office, placed her head in her hands, and began weeping. A few moments later, there was a knock at the door. It was Kwan, and he had been moved by her kind heart. He said, "No one has ever cared for me before; if this has something to do with your Christ, I want to know about Him."

What made the difference? Dr. Marilyn Hellenberg profoundly believed that every one of her students was created in the image of God and that they had unlimited potential in His sight. She believed in Kwan's potential, saw him through Christ's eyes, and prayed for him.

People in crisis or transition are often open to spiritual realities. Maybe they have been diagnosed with a serious illness or experienced a broken relationship or of the loss of a job. These crossroads present an opportunity to give a personal testimony about God's faithfulness, share a promise from His Word, or offer a short prayer. These sincere gestures build friendships, and as has always been the case, we win our friends to Christ, not our enemies. First comes friendship, then Christian friendship, and eventually, a Seventh-day Adventist Christian friend is made. When this is your life's goal, God will lead you on an exciting journey of discovering the lost and leading them to a saving relationship with Him.

---

1. Ellen G. White, *Steps to Christ* (Nampa, ID: Pacific Press®, 1999), 80.
2. White, *Steps to Christ*, 83.

Two

The Power of Personal Testimony

Pete was raised in a Seventh-day Adventist home. He attended church throughout his childhood, but during his teen years, he drifted away. Although he developed a successful business career, something was missing in his life. There was a barrenness of soul, an emptiness that could not be filled with money and things. Now in his mid-forties, he was searching for something more, something better than what he had. Unfortunately, he did not know what that something was.

Sensing his inner struggle, his mother gave him a copy of the book *Steps to Christ*. As he read the first chapter, "God's Love for Man," the Holy Spirit touched his heart, and he came to view God with new eyes. Here was Someone who loved him more than he could have ever imagined. Here was a God who looked beyond his faults, his sins, and the mistakes of his past life. A God who met his deepest heart needs. For the first time in his life, the plan of salvation became real. Heartbroken over his wayward life, he discovered forgiveness, grace, and freedom from condemnation at the Cross. In short, Pete was a new man in Christ. The Bible became a precious testament to the love of God. Prayer became a meaningful conversation with a Friend who cared. Everything was new.

Here is the amazing thing. Pete could not keep quiet about

his newfound joy in Christ. He shared it with his wife. His work associates noticed the change, too, as he unashamedly recounted his conversion story. When Christ fills hearts, lives are changed, and the converted cannot remain silent. Indeed, the most significant witness and the most persuasive testimony for the gospel is a changed life.

The power of personal testimony

There is incredible power in a personal testimony. When an individual accepts Christ, the person's life is dramatically changed, and people notice. Some conversions are sudden and instantaneous. You have undoubtedly heard of thrilling conversions: drug addicts accepting Christ; alcoholics transformed by grace; self-centered, materialistic business leaders changed by God's love; or rebellious teenagers converted. But more often than not, the Holy Spirit works gently and gradually on human hearts.

Many reared in godly Christian homes have a precious story to tell. Though they may have never really rebelled against Christ, they also were never fully committed to Him either. Their heart's void senses the moving of the Holy Spirit, and they commit themselves totally to God. This quiet conversion is just as powerful as the more dramatic conversion stories. No one is born a Christian, and as Jeremiah candidly reminds us, "The heart is deceitful above all things, and desperately wicked; who can know it?" (Jeremiah 17:9). The apostle Paul echoes the sad human condition: "For all have sinned and fall short of the glory of God" (Romans 3:23).

Since each of us is a sinner by nature and by choice, we all need the grace of God. Conversion is not for a select few. It is for everyone. It follows that every person saved by grace has a unique story to tell. Your story is not my story, and my story is not your story. Each of us, redeemed by God's grace and charmed by His love, has a personal testimony to share with the world. You may wonder, *What is so great about my testimony?* This is a fair question, and the answer involves your witness. Your conversion story may seem bland to you, but it will connect with someone God places in your life. Your testimony will powerfully draw new believers to the peace, forgiveness, and assurance you have experienced.

The Bible shows that God moves dramatically, but it also describes a daily progression of drawing nearer and nearer to Jesus. Ellen White beautifully describes this conversion process in *Steps to Christ*: "A person may not be able to tell the exact time or place or trace all the chain of circumstances in the process of conversion; but this does not prove him to be unconverted."[1]

Like Nicodemus, your conversion experience may have been a gradual process, a gentle wooing of the Holy Spirit. Or, like the thief on the cross, it may be dramatic, a miraculous change at a watershed moment in your life. Whatever the case, there is a story to tell—a story of salvation freely offered in Christ. His power to change lives is a prominent theme in the New Testament, and whatever the circumstances, a new life in Jesus is profound and lasting.

The first missionaries

Here is your Bible trivia quiz for today: Whom did Jesus send out as His first missionary? Was it Peter, or possibly James and John? Maybe Thomas, Philip, or one of the other disciples? The answer may surprise you. It was none of the names listed above. The first missionary Christ commissioned was a demon-possessed man transformed by His grace. This unlikely witness had a powerful impact on Decapolis, ten towns on the eastern shore of the Sea of Galilee. The demoniac had been hopelessly possessed for years. He terrorized the region, striking fear in the hearts of local villagers. Yet deep down in his heart, there was a longing for something better, a longing that demonic forces could not quench.

Despite the demonic forces that held this poor man in bondage, Mark 5 records that when he saw Jesus, he "ran and worshiped Him" (Mark 5:6). The Scripture says that this man was tormented and possessed by a "legion" of demons. According to the *Archaeological Study Bible*, a legion is "the largest single unit in the Roman army. . . . A legion at full strength consisted of about 6,000 soldiers."[2] In the New Testament, the term represents a vast, or huge, number. Jesus never lost a battle with the demons, no matter how many there were. Christ is our all-powerful, victorious Lord. The forces of darkness tremble at the approach of the King of the universe.

Once the demoniac was delivered, he was found "sitting and clothed and in his right mind" (Mark 5:15). Where did he get the clothes? It is likely the disciples shared their outer garments with him. He now sat attentively at the feet of Jesus, listening to His words, eagerly absorbing spiritual truths. He was physically, mentally, emotionally, and spiritually whole. His one desire now was to follow Jesus. He longed to become one of Jesus' disciples.

In verse 18, Mark's Gospel records that he "begged" Jesus to allow him to enter the boat and journey with Him. *Begged* is a strong word. It indicates a passionate desire. It can be translated "beseeched," "implored," or "entreated." It is full of emotion. It is asking with intensity. It is a persistent urging. The transformed demoniac desired only one thing: to be with the One who delivered him from the clutches of the evil one. He could sing with the modern songwriter, "Amazing grace. . . . My chains are gone, I've been set free."[3]

Jesus' response is as amazing as the demoniac's conversion. Jesus knew that this converted, transformed demoniac could do more in that region than He or His disciples. The prejudice against Christ was high in this Gentile region, and the citizens would be more likely to listen to one of their own, especially one with a reputation like this demoniac. While one can turn away from the most explicit biblical teaching, it is much more difficult to resist the testimony of a changed life. Christ knew that after the inhabitants of Decapolis heard the testimony of the transformed demoniac, they would be ready for His message when He returned later.

And so, Jesus said, "Go home to your friends, and tell them what great things the Lord has done for you, and how He has had compassion on you" (Mark 5:19). The man's response was immediate. "And he departed and began to proclaim in Decapolis all that Jesus had done for him; and all marveled" (verse 20). The Greek word that is translated "proclaim" is *kerusso* and can be translated "to herald" or "to publish." In the brief time that the demoniac spent with Jesus, his life was so radically changed that he had a story to tell. He had a testimony to give. He had an incredible experience to share. We can only imagine the impact of his testimony on the thousands of people in the Gadara region.[4] When Jesus returned some nine or ten months later, the minds of this largely Gentile population were ready to receive Him.

This story teaches an eternal truth that must not be overlooked. It should not be overshadowed by the miraculous, sensational, and somewhat dramatic conversion of the demoniac. Christ desires to use all who come to Him. The demoniac did not have the advantage of spending time with Jesus, as the disciples did. He did not have the opportunity of listening to His sermons or witnessing His miracles, but he did have the one indispensable ingredient for experiencing a changed life: he had personal knowledge of the living Christ. He had a heart filled with love for his Master. This is the essence of New Testament witnessing. As Ellen White so aptly states,

Our confession of His faithfulness is Heaven's chosen agency for revealing Christ to the world. We are to acknowledge His grace as made known through the holy men of old; but that which will be most effectual is the testimony of our own experience. We are witnesses for God as we reveal in ourselves the working of a power that is divine. Every individual has a life distinct from all others, and an experience differing essentially from theirs. God desires that our praise shall ascend to Him, marked by our own individuality. These precious acknowledgments to the praise of the glory of His grace, when supported by a Christ-like life, have an irresistible power that works for the salvation of souls.[5]

The Power of Personal Testimony

New Testament believers witnessed for Christ through the uniqueness of their personalities. Their distinctive encounters with Christ led them to enthusiastically share Him with others. The circumstances of their conversion may have been different, but the results were the same: hearts transformed by God's love. When Christ changes your life and you are transformed by His grace, you cannot be silent. Filled with Christ's love, John, the beloved apostle, testifies, "That which was from the beginning, which we have heard, which we have seen with our eyes, which we have looked upon, and our hands have handled, concerning the Word of life—the life was manifested, and we have seen, and bear witness, and declare to you that eternal life" (1 John 1:1, 2). Here is John's point: The disciples were not proclaiming something theoretical. They were sharing a Christ whom they knew personally—the Christ of relationships. Their personal encounter with the living Christ was the power of New Testament witnessing.

Consider the experience of the women who came to the tomb to embalm Christ's body. They last saw Jesus as His bloodied body was taken down from the cross. Think of the despair and disappointment they must have experienced at that moment. The Sabbath hours must have been the most miserable they had ever spent. Christ was dead. With their own eyes, they saw their dreams dashed.

Now with fearful hearts, anxious about the future, they approached the tomb, hoping to slip past the Roman guards and anoint the body of their Lord. They still had no idea how they would move the stone that blocked the tomb's entrance, but somehow their fear did not paralyze their faith. They didn't know how it would happen, but they believed that the stone would be rolled away. They were simply doing what needed to be done and trusting God to bless their mission.

Arriving at the tomb, they are amazed. The Roman soldiers are gone, nowhere to be seen. The stone is rolled away, and to their surprise, the tomb is empty. Startled by an angelic being, they stand agape, listening to his announcement, "He is risen. . . . Go quickly and tell His disciples" (Matthew 28:6, 7). The record states, "So they went out quickly from the tomb with fear and great joy, and ran to bring His disciples word" (verse 8). As they run to tell their story, the resurrected Lord meets them and exclaims, "Rejoice! . . . Go and tell My brethren to go to Galilee, and there they will see Me" (verses 9, 10). You see, good news is for sharing. Hearts filled with God's grace and charmed by His love cannot be silent. In the presence of the resurrected Christ, sorrow is turned to joy. Their hearts overflow with gladness. They cannot wait to tell the story about their resurrected Lord. They are forever changed. The resurrected Christ has appeared to them, and they must tell the story. From this moment forward, the recurring New Testament theme is one of witness. The apostles and the disciples witnessed about a Christ they knew, one whom they had personally experienced.

They were not false witnesses. Suppose you were called to a court of law as a witness of some accident or crime. Let's further assume that you were not present at the scene and made up a story to assist a friend. You could be imprisoned for lying to the court. The judge and jury are only interested in witnesses who personally experienced the events. They want genuine witnesses, not impostors.

Only genuine, authentic Christianity can capture the attention of this generation. Unless we have had a personal, real experience with Jesus, our witness will fall on deaf ears. We cannot share a Christ we do not know.

Peter, John, and other New Testament believers spoke with conviction from converted hearts: "For we cannot but speak the things which we have seen and heard" (Acts 4:20). Before the cross, Peter was a vacillating, self-assured disciple. After the crucifixion and resurrection of Christ, he was a changed man. Before the cross, John was one of the "Sons of Thunder," a brash and strong-willed youth. After the resurrection, he, too, was a changed man—telling the story of transforming grace.

The truth of grace's transforming power brings us to an important point. Our witness is not primarily about our previous goodness or badness before we met Jesus. It is all about Jesus. It is about His love, His grace, His mercy, His pardon, and His eternal power to save. The apostle Paul never tired of testifying about what Christ did for him, but he did not focus on how bad he was. He focused on how good God was. He rejoiced in the good news of the gospel. One renowned preacher is reported to have said that the gospel "tells rebellious men that God is reconciled; that justice is satisfied; that sin has been atoned for; that the judgment of the guilty may be revoked, the condemnation of the sinner cancelled, the curse of the law blotted out, the gates of hell closed, the portals of heaven opened wide, the power of sin subdued, the guilty conscience healed, the broken heart comforted, the sorrow and misery of the fall undone."[6]

The essence of all New Testament witness is the gracious good news of the salvation so freely offered in Christ. The apostle Paul admonishes us to look to Jesus, "the author and finisher of our faith" (Hebrews 12:2). What do we see when we look to Him? We see the Jesus who redeemed us. He has forgiven our sins. He has taken away our guilt. He has silenced the accusing voice in our head. We see the Jesus who said to the woman caught in adultery, "Go and sin no more" (John 8:11). We see the Jesus who said to the dying thief, "You will be with Me in paradise" (Luke 23:43). We see the Jesus who, dying on the cross, cried to the Father, "Forgive them; for they know not what they do" (verse 34, KJV). We see the Jesus who transformed Peter from a loud-mouthed fisherman to a powerful preacher. We see the Jesus who delivered the demoniacs from bondage. We see the all-sufficient Christ who delivers us from both the penalty and the power of sin. In Him, we have peace, freedom, and hope.

It is this personal encounter with Christ that changes us from passive spectators to active witnesses. It is the transforming grace of God that shines from our lives to lighten the darkness of this world. The love that flows from Calvary's cross overflows in our hearts to others. Good news is for sharing. As Ellen White states in *Steps to Christ*, "When the love of Christ is enshrined in the heart, like sweet fragrance it cannot be hidden. Its holy influence will be felt by all with whom we come in contact. The spirit of Christ in the heart is like a spring in the desert, flowing to refresh all and making those who are ready to perish, eager to drink of the water of life."[7] The water of life has quenched our thirsty souls, and we can no longer be silent. We have a story to tell, a testimony to give, and a message to share.

Has Christ changed your life? Have you personally experienced His abounding grace? Are you amazed by His love? Why not ask Him to lead you on an adventure in mission? It will be the most exciting journey of your life. There is someone in your sphere of influence that He can reach through you. It may be a family member, a work associate, a friend, or a casual acquaintance, but if your life is open to the promptings of the Holy Spirit, you will be thrilled at the opportunities that present themselves. Doors will miraculously open. Why not spend a few minutes right now to consider Christ's incredible love for you? Ask Him to bring someone into your life with whom you can share His love.

1. Ellen G. White, *Steps to Christ* (Nampa, ID: Pacific Press®, 1999), 57.

2. *NIV Archaeological Study Bible* (Grand Rapids, MI: Zondervan, 2005), 1633.

3. Stan Roto Walker, David Pritchard-blunt, Christ Tomlin, and Louie Giglio, "Amazing Grace (My Chains Are Gone)," from Chris Tomlin, *Songs of the Morning*, lyrics © Sony/ATV Music Publishing LLC, 2006.

4. Ellen G. White, *The Desire of Ages* (Mountain View, CA: Pacific Press®, 1940), 340, 341.

5. White, *Desire of Ages*, 347.

6. A. B. Simpson, *The Christ of the 40 Days* (New Kensington, PA: Whitaker House, 2014).

7. White, *Steps to Christ*, 77.

Three

Seeing People Through Jesus' Eyes

I met Ted one afternoon over forty years ago in a small mill town in southeastern Massachusetts. Our evangelistic teams were visiting homes door-to-door, encouraging people to study the Bible. Ted expressed interest in future Bible studies and invited us to return the next week. As we began our weekly Bible studies, Ted made one thing clear. This was his home, and he would do what he liked during our Bible studies. Often, during the early studies, Ted lit up a cigarette. At times, he drank his favorite beer. If there was ever a Bible study interest that appeared unlikely to respond, it was Ted. Yet deep in his heart, he longed for something better. As the Bible studies progressed, the Holy Spirit worked powerfully in his life. The day came when he gave up his smoking and drinking. Over a period of months, he accepted the truths of Scripture, began attending church, and was eventually baptized. For years, Ted remained a faithful Seventh-day Adventist Christian. Jesus often surprises us, and the unlikeliest prospects become the most committed Christians.

The theme of this chapter, seeing people through Jesus' eyes, focuses on the significance of seeing everyone as winnable for Christ, regardless of their circumstances. Jesus saw people not as they were but as they might become, refined and ennobled by His grace. He saw their potential for the kingdom of God. He perceived divine longings in the heart of each person. He believed that no one was beyond the grace of God. Jesus did not merely look at people; He perceived their needs, their sorrows, and their deepest longings.

When we see people through Jesus' eyes, we see them as winnable for Christ because they were created in His image. Despite the circumstances of their lives, they have an inner desire to know Him. This desire was present in the Samaritan woman, the Ethiopian eunuch, the thief on the cross, the Roman centurion, and a host of other New Testament seekers. There is an emptiness of the soul without Christ. There is a barrenness of spirit without Jesus. Life has little real meaning apart from Him. He is the Bread of Life that satisfies our hungry hearts. He is the Water of Life that quenches our thirsty souls. He is the solid Rock that forms the foundation for our faith. He is the Light that shines in our darkness. He is the one who takes us from despair to the delights of discipleship. He is the almighty, all-powerful Son of God who can radically change any life.

Recognizing this eternal truth enables us to see people with new eyes. Whether they realize it or not, they have a God-shaped vacuum in their lives. Beyond their felt needs, they have an eternal longing to know God, a hidden hunger of the soul. Twenty-first-century men and women are starved for a knowledge of God.

It is God's plan that each one of us seizes the opportunities around us and leads our friends to Jesus. Many people will never come unless we bring them. In the New Testament, more than half of Jesus' healing miracles were performed for people who were brought to Him by someone else. God delights in using people to reach people.

At times, our prejudice gets in the way of our witness. Our preconceived ideas about others limit our ability to reach them. But do not think that people around you have no interest in spiritual things. Set that myth aside and understand that people are genuinely interested in spiritual matters. Like Jesus, view people as winnable, and watch them respond to the Holy Spirit.

Jesus heals the blind man at Bethsaida

To better understand the idea of viewing each person as winnable, let us consider Christ's two-stage healing of the blind man at Bethsaida. First, it is important to note the location of this healing. Though its exact location is debated, Bethsaida is believed to be located on the northern shore of the Sea of Galilee. The city is frequently mentioned in the Gospels, along with Jerusalem and Capernaum. It was here that Jesus called Philip, Peter, and Andrew to become His disciples. The name *Bethsaida* is translated "house or dwelling place of fish." Jesus called His first disciples to be fishers of men in a fishing village on the shores of Galilee. In the healing of the blind man at Bethsaida, Jesus reveals compassion for human suffering.

In Mark 8:22, the Gospel narrative records, "Then He came to Bethsaida; and they brought a blind man to Him, and begged Him to touch him." Note that the man was brought by his friends. Being blind, he could not have found Jesus by himself. Wandering in the darkness, he would have no idea where to go. Today, many people are in the same predicament, wandering in spiritual darkness, in need of someone to guide them to Jesus. The second thing to notice about this text is that the blind man's friends "begged" Jesus to heal the man. The Greek word translated "begged," *parakaleō*, is a strong word. It means to ask with passion, to earnestly plead for, or vigorously appeal. Successful soul winners see people as winnable and cooperate with the Holy Spirit in bringing them to Jesus.

Jesus healed this blind man in two stages for important reasons. Since it is the only time in the Gospels that Jesus' healing miracle was not instantaneous, there must be some significance in this miracle not seen in other places in Scripture. First, a careful study of the details of the story reveals Jesus' special concern for people. Have you ever walked out of a dark room into the bright light? For a moment, you were blinded. It takes time for your eyes to adjust to light if you have been in the dark. If you were blind, a sudden bright light would affect you even more. Jesus healed the man in two stages so that his eyes would gradually adapt to the light. Jesus is gracious. He understands our condition and lovingly ministers to our needs.

In addition to His compassion for this blind man, it may be that Jesus was teaching more profound lessons to His disciples regarding effective witnessing. He desired them to recognize that there were needy people all around them who would be open to the gospel if their physical needs were met first. Christ's method of soul winning was to meet people's felt needs so that their minds would be open to divine realities.

As we share the light of God's truth with our friends, it is well to remember that "the path of the just is like the shining sun, that shines ever brighter unto the perfect day" (Proverbs 4:18). Just as the sun gradually rises, dispelling the darkness, so the light of God's truth gradually illuminates our minds until we walk in its full light. However, light can be blinding as well as enlightening. You will recall that Jesus said to His disciples, "I still have many things to say to you, but you cannot bear them now. However, when He, the Spirit of truth, has come, He will guide you into all truth" (John 16:12, 13). An eternal principle of soul winning is to reveal biblical truth gradually, no faster than people can grasp it. Jesus understood this principle and, in the two-stage healing of this blind man, left His disciples a vivid example of how to present truth.

It is also possible that Jesus desired to reveal to His followers that each one of us needs the second touch. Too often, we are partially blind. We see people as "trees walking around." When the Holy Spirit causes the scales to fall from our eyes, we will see those around us more clearly. Significantly, Mark notes that Jesus "put His hands on his eyes again and made him look up. And he was restored and saw everyone clearly" (Mark 8:25). The Greek word translated "clearly" is *delaugos*, which is better translated as "radiantly" or "in full light." When Christ heals our spiritual blindness, we see others as Christ sees them in the full light of His love.

The second touch is the anointing of the Holy Spirit so that we see every human being as winnable for Christ. Every individual is a candidate for the kingdom of God. All are potential citizens of heaven. Through the cross of Calvary, Jesus has redeemed all humankind. It is our role to share His amazing grace so that people can accept the salvation He freely offers. Since Christ sees all humanity through the eyes of divine compassion, He invites us to view them through the lens of His grace.

Jesus ministers to a Samaritan woman

With divine compassion, it was through the lens of grace that Jesus viewed the Samaritan woman. The animosity between the Jews and Samaritans at this time was high, and the woman was an unlikely prospect for the kingdom of God. Purposefully, Jesus chose a route through Samaria, the most direct way from Jerusalem to Galilee. Because of their dislike of the Samaritans, the Jews avoided this road. They regularly took the longer and circuitous route through the Jordan Valley. John 4:4 states that Jesus "needed to go through Samaria." Unfazed by the bigotry of the Jews, He "needed" to go to Samaria because He had a divine appointment at the well with a Samaritan woman, an appointment that would make an eternal difference in her life.

Jesus desired to break down the walls of prejudice between the Jews and the Samaritans. He wanted to show His disciples that the Samaritans were open to the gospel. He observed this troubled woman through the eyes of divine compassion, noting that she came to the well at noon, the hottest part of the day. The noon hour was a strange time to come to draw water. The village women went in the early morning hours. There they gathered, socializing as they drew their water supply for the day. Evidently, this woman wanted to avoid the other women, preferring not to hear their remarks about her lifestyle.

She was probably embarrassed. Her profligacy made her an outcast. She was well known and wanted to avoid contact as much as possible. Her sole desire was to gather her daily supply of water and quickly return home. Intent on her mission, she was surprised to find this Galilean Jewish stranger at the well.

She was even more amazed when He spoke to her. The Jews had no dealings with the Samaritans, and when Jesus asked her for a favor, she could not refuse. In the barren desert lands of the Middle East, it is still believed that water is a gift of God. To deny a cup of water to a weary traveler is an offense against the Almighty.

Gently, almost imperceptibly, Jesus broke down the barriers that separated them. He won her confidence and then appealed directly to her inner longings to be guilt-free and enjoy the promise of eternal life. She recognized Jesus as a righteous man, acknowledging that He was more than a religious teacher. As the Holy Spirit awakened divine impulses within her soul, she sensed that Jesus must be the Messiah (verses 11, 15, 19, 25).

Excited with the chance encounter, she forgets the reason she came to the well and runs to tell the story of her visit with Christ. Her testimony produces a spiritual revival in the entire area (verses 39–41). When the disciples return from their journey to buy food, Jesus tells them that the Samaritans are open and receptive to the gospel. For the disciples, this was almost unbelievable and, quite predictably, has remained challenging in every generation. Human nature is not inclined to expect God in all people and all cultures. But keep your eyes open, and you will see the providential working of the Holy Spirit in the lives of those whom you may not expect to receive the gospel (verses 35–38). Often there are people all around you who are open to the gospel.

Berry picking and soul winning

The idea that the gospel is for all people is beautifully illustrated in a fascinating dream given to Ellen White. On the night of September 29, 1886, she had a dream about berry picking and soul winning.[1] Along with a large group of young people, a horse-drawn wagon carried supplies to a location filled with whortleberry bushes. Whortleberries, also known as huckleberries, are either blue or red and quite delicious. They are healthy, too, since they are filled with antioxidants.

Ellen noticed the bushes filled with berries close to the wagon and began to pick them. Soon she had filled two buckets full. The others in her group scattered and came back after a while with empty buckets. She admonished them that while they were looking for berries a distance away from the wagon, there were plenty of berries right before them if they would only open their eyes to see them. Her heavenly messenger impressed upon her mind that her dream contained a vital lesson about winning others to Christ. She explained the meaning of the dream in these words, "You should be diligent, first to pick the berries nearest you, and then to search for those who are farther away; after that you can return and work near by again, and thus you will be successful."[2] In light of this counsel, ask God to give you divinely enlightened eyes to see the people in your sphere of influence, people ready to receive God's truth.

Start where you are

Jesus urged the disciples to begin sharing the gospel where they were. There is no better place to start than the place where you are. The disciples were to share the gospel first in Jerusalem, Judea, and Samaria, and then in the uttermost parts of the earth. There are people all around us looking for the peace and purpose that only Christ can give. Jesus invites us to begin sharing His love in our families, our neighborhoods, our workplaces, and our communities.

Andrew began with his own family and shared the gospel with his brother Peter. On another occasion, he developed a friendship with a little boy. He gained this boy's confidence, and when there was a need, this lad gave his lunch to Andrew, who, in turn, gave it to Jesus for the miracle of feeding five thousand people. Little in the hands of Jesus is much, and small in the hands of Jesus is great. Jesus always begins with what He has. He fed five thousand people on the hillsides of Galilee with only five loaves and two fish. Andrew was not as outgoing as Peter. He did not have the same leadership qualities, but he was an introducer. Every time we read about Andrew, we find him introducing somebody to Jesus. In John 12, when some Greeks are longing to meet Jesus, Andrew and Philip are the disciples that lead them to the Savior.

The Gospels are filled with stories of Jesus sharing God's love with one person at a time. A Jewish scribe, a Roman tax collector, a Canaanite woman, a Jewish religious leader, and a young thief all experienced His loving touch. God's grace transformed them.

Think about your sphere of influence. With whom might you share God's love? Who among your family or friends might be most receptive to the gospel? Start there and ask God to impress you with those who are seeking Him. You may be surprised at the results. He will open doors of opportunity to share with those who you thought would never be receptive.

---

1. Ellen G. White, *Christian Service* (Washington, DC: Review and Herald®, 1947), 46–49.

2. White, *Christian Service*, 49.

Four

Interceding for Others

When my Catholic mother and Protestant father were married, he promised the priest that he would bring up their children Catholic. However, it turned out that God had other plans. My father worked the night shift in a factory producing staplers, much like the ones used in offices and schools. The day shift foreman, Al Lyons, was a Seventh-day Adventist, and over the years, they developed a close friendship. Each evening, when Dad reported to Al to learn the night shift priorities, Al would share his faith with him. After two years of intense Bible study with Al and others, Dad was baptized into the Seventh-day Adventist Church. Immediately, he began praying for his family, and God answered his prayers in a remarkable way. A few years later, I was baptized, and in time, my mother and sisters followed.

From the beginning, my dad's prayers for his family never ceased. Fifty years later, the image of my father on his knees, praying for me, is still vivid in my mind. Dad loved his family, and he wanted them to be in heaven together. He was an earnest prayer warrior.

Prayer is a powerful weapon
In the great controversy between good and evil, intercessory

prayer is a powerful weapon (2 Corinthians 10:4, 5). It is not merely a pious platitude to make us feel warm inside. It is, as Ellen White says, "the opening of the heart to God as to a friend."[1] It is sharing with Him your joys and sorrows, struggles and victories, dreams and disappointments. It is in prayer that we connect with God on the deepest level. It is through intercession that we engage in spiritual warfare and plead with the Almighty for the salvation of people we love. It is in those quiet moments of prayer that our hearts are knit together with the heart of God. It is through prayer that God gives us the wisdom to reach those around us, and it is through prayer that the Holy Spirit works powerfully to influence their lives.

God is doing everything He can to reach people without our prayers, but He is gracious and never violates their freedom of choice. However, our prayers make a difference because there are ground rules in the conflict between good and evil. One of the eternal laws of the universe is that God has given to every human being the freedom of choice. All the demons of darkness cannot force us to sin, and all the heavenly angels would never coerce us to do right. God voluntarily limits Himself by our choices. He does not use force to motivate our service to Him.

When we intercede for someone else, it enables God to work in ways that He could not work if we did not pray. In the cosmic conflict between the forces of heaven and the legions of darkness, God honors our freedom of choice to pray for another by powerfully working on their behalf. He will never coerce the will, but He does send His Spirit to move on their hearts in more powerful ways. He does send heavenly angels from worlds afar to beat back the forces of darkness so the individual we are praying for will have a clear mind to make the right decision. Under the inspiration of the Holy Spirit, Ellen White declares the efficacy of intercessory prayer in this remarkable statement: "Ministering angels are waiting about the throne to instantly obey the mandate of Jesus Christ to answer every prayer offered in earnest, living faith."[2]

As our prayers ascend to the throne of God, Jesus commissions heavenly angels to instantly descend to earth. He empowers them to beat back the forces of darkness that are battling for the mind of the individual for whom we are interceding. The individual has the freedom to choose Christ or Satan. Our prayers do not force or manipulate the will; they provide the best opportunity for the individual to see the issues clearly, providing them the best possibility of choosing eternal life.

Prayer opens our hearts to divine influences, and our prayers open doors of opportunity for God to work more powerfully on another person's behalf. He respects our freedom of choice and pours out His Spirit through us to influence them for His kingdom. He releases the powers of heaven on their behalf. Our prayers become the channel through which God powerfully influences others for eternal life.

A powerful passage on intercessory prayer

One of the most powerful passages in the Bible on intercessory prayer is found in 1 John 5:14–16. The passage begins with the assurance that God hears our prayers. "Now this is the confidence that we have in Him, that if we ask anything according to His will, He hears us" (verse 14). The word *confidence* means "strong assurance." It conveys a sense of certainty. Confidence is the opposite of doubt and uncertainty.

Notice that our confidence is not in our prayers; it is in the God who answers our prayers. God's promise to answer prayer is not without conditions. When our will is molded by God's will, we can have absolute assurance that He will hear us. It is always God's will to forgive our sins. It is always God's will to give us victory over the power of evil. It is always God's will to provide us with the gift of salvation, and it is always God's will to lead those we are praying for to knowledge of His Word. Indeed, those we are praying for have a choice to accept or reject the salvation Christ so freely offers, but God is working through our prayers to do everything possible to save them.

By faith, we believe that God's promises are true. By faith, we believe that He will answer our prayers. By faith, we believe He is working in ways we cannot see and in ways we do not understand, seeking to save those we are praying for. First John 5:16 describes what happens when we pray. It draws the curtain aside and gives us a glimpse of God's divine activity through our prayers. "If anyone sees his brother sinning a sin which does not lead to death, he will ask, and He will give him life for those who commit sin not leading to death." Here John lists two kinds of sin: sins that lead to death and sins that do not lead to death.

Most Bible scholars understand the sin that leads to death as the unpardonable sin. John does not encourage us to pray for that sin. However, he does encourage us to pray for individuals who have not committed the unpardonable sin. As we ask God to save them, He gives us "life for those who commit sin not leading to death" (verse 16).

What does it mean that God gives to the praying one, the intercessor, life for others? The *Seventh-day Adventist Bible Commentary* suggests that "Christ shall give the praying Christian life to pass on to those sinners who have not finally hardened their hearts. . . . The Christian has no power apart from the Saviour; so, in the end, it is Christ who gives the life, though the intercessory prayer may have been the instrument through which that life has been granted."[3] Our prayers become the channel for the very life of God to flow to hearts longing for salvation. The river of the water of life flows through our prayers to touch the lives of others. The power of our prayers for others is a fantastic thought. At times we scarcely recognize the power of intercessory prayer. It is even more powerful when two or three people gather together for prayer. Here are two significant statements from God's last-day messenger: "Why do not believers feel a deeper, more earnest concern for those who are out of Christ? Why do not two or three meet together and plead with God for the salvation of some special one, and then for still another?"[4] Elsewhere, she quotes Matthew 18:19, 20, adding an important comment:

> "If two of you shall agree on earth as touching any thing that they shall ask, it shall be done for them of My Father which is in heaven. For where two or three are

gathered together in My name, there am I in the midst of them" (Matthew 18:19, 20). "Ask of Me, and I will answer your requests."

The promise is made on condition that the united prayers of the church are offered, and in answer to these prayers there may be expected a power greater than that which comes in response to private prayer. The power given will be proportionate to the unity of the members and their love for God and for one another.[5]

Intercessory prayer makes a difference. When we pray alone, God answers our prayers, but when we pray together for others, there is "a power greater." The early church experienced this power when they prayed together in the upper room (Acts 1:13, 14).

Jesus' prayer life

The Gospels detail in quite specific terms the prayer life of Jesus. One of the facets of Jesus' life that stands out in bold relief is the times He spent alone with God in prayer. The Gospel of Luke focuses on the prayer life of Jesus more than any other book in the Bible. Luke was a Gentile physician, committed to Christ, who longed to share the eternal truths of salvation with both Jew and Gentile.

The Gospel of Luke was written to a growing Christian community around A.D. 60. It emphasizes our relationship with God and one another. Significantly, it is addressed to Theophilus, which means "lover of God" or "a friend of God." The purpose of Luke is to lead each reader to become "God's friend." It is also fascinating to note that Luke's Gospel highlights Jesus' prayer life. The Greeks believed that the gods were separate from and quite distant from humanity. They had no concept of human beings developing a relationship with the gods. In his Gospel, Luke presents a revolutionary idea. Jesus, the divine Son of God, dwelt in human flesh and, in His humanity, developed an intimate relationship with God in prayer.

Luke states it this way: "So He Himself often withdrew into

the wilderness and prayed" (Luke 5:16). In chapter 9, Luke adds, "And it happened, as He was alone praying . . ." (verse 18). Matthew describes several times that Jesus withdrew from the crowds to pray. When the destiny of the world trembled in the balance, Jesus pled with God in Gethsemane for strength to face the enormous challenge ahead (Matthew 26:36–39).

Mark's Gospel begins with a precise description of Jesus' prayer life. After a Sabbath of hectic activity in Capernaum, Jesus arose early and "went out and departed to a solitary place, and there He prayed" (Mark 1:35). There are three things to note about the specifics of Jesus' prayer life. First, He had a time to pray. Often, the early morning found Him spending quiet time alone with God. Second, He had a place to pray. Jesus had His favorite spots where He could commune with the Father away from the hectic activity of the crowds that so commonly pressed in around Him. Third, Jesus' secret prayers were not necessarily silent prayers. Three times in the Gethsemane prayer, Matthew's Gospel records that Jesus fell on His face "saying" (Matthew 26:39, 42, 44). The book of Hebrews records that Jesus "offered up prayers and supplications, with vehement cries and tears to Him who was able to save Him from death, and was heard because of His godly fear" (Hebrews 5:7).

On one occasion, the disciples heard Christ praying and were so moved that they requested He teach them to pray (Luke 11:1). Ellen White adds this insightful statement: "Learn to pray aloud where only God can hear you."[6] Some people are concerned about praying out loud because they are afraid Satan will hear them and learn the content of their prayers. They reason that because Satan cannot read our thoughts, it is better to pray silently. Praying silently in our minds is certainly appropriate, but the silence can also cause our minds to wander.

There is something special about praying out loud that keeps us focused. When we have an appointed time to meet with God and a designated prayer place, our audible prayer becomes more meaningful, and our prayer life is enhanced. We don't have to worry about Satan hearing our prayers because at the sound of earnest prayer, Satan's whole host trembles and flees. When we seek God in prayer, heavenly angels encircle us. The evil angels are beaten back, and we can commune with God in confidence.

When we pray for others, our prayers unite with Christ's prayers, our mighty Intercessor, at the throne of God. He immediately employs all the resources of heaven to positively influence the ones for whom we are praying. Jesus prayed for Peter by name. He prayed that Peter would experience a deep conversion. (See Luke 22:31, 32.) Jesus' prayers were answered, and Peter became the mighty preacher of Pentecost (Acts 2).

The apostle Paul prayed for the Ephesian, Colossian, and Philippian churches by name. He also often prayed for his gospel companions by name. They were in his heart and on his lips in prayer. Along with Jesus, the apostle Paul interceded for those with whom he labored and those whom he labored for.

Arguably, one of the great giants of the Old Testament was Daniel. His intercession for Israel is recorded in Daniel 9 and 10. Intercessory prayer is biblical and powerful. Daniel's heartfelt prayers are an example to the church today of the power of intercession. Intercessory prayer is part of God's plan to transform our lives and reach lost people.

Would you like to have a more vibrant prayer life? Would you like to become a mighty intercessor for God? Here are a few practical steps you can follow:

1. Set aside a specific time and place to seek God for the salvation of others.
2. Ask God to impress you with people who need prayer. Spend time thinking of those within your sphere of influence who need your prayers. The Holy Spirit will impress you with those who are struggling and in need of prayer.
3. Make a list of those you are impressed to pray for. Follow the method of Jesus and pray for them aloud, by name.
4. As you seek God in prayer, invite others to join you in your times of intercession. Jesus invited Peter, James, and John into His inner circle for times of earnest

prayer. Praying together with others is a powerful method of staying focused in prayer. Our prayers unite with Christ's prayers, and all of Heaven answers.

In the late 1980s, I was conducting a series of evangelistic meetings in London. Each day we commuted into the city by train for an hour from our home in Saint Albans. We taught in the mornings, visited interested people in the afternoon, and preached each evening. After the meeting, we took the subway to the train and journeyed home. Working twelve-hour days for weeks, I was getting exhausted. One day, as I was slowly climbing the stairs to begin another day of teaching at the New Gallery Centre, the headquarters for our meetings, I glanced into a side room and noticed a group of my students praying. I paused for a moment and listened to their prayers. My heart was touched. My soul was moved. My spirits were lifted as they prayed, "Dear Lord, Pastor Mark looks very tired this week; please give him extra energy." Their prayers brought new strength to my life that day, and I bounded up the stairs, ready to teach. It is a wonderful thing to know that someone is praying for you.

When you know your spouse is praying for you, it brings a sense of peace to your life. When children know that their parents are praying for them, it brings stability to their lives and provides them with a solid foundation for their faith. When you have friends who are praying for you, it bonds you to them in the divine cords of love. It is a wonderful thing to know that someone who cares is praying for you, but here is something even more incredible: to know that Jesus is praying for you in heaven right now. Your name is on His lips; your concerns are in His heart; and your anxieties, fears, and worries matter to Him.

1. Ellen G. White, *Steps to Christ* (Nampa, ID: Pacific Press®, 1999), 93.

2. Ellen G. White, *Selected Messages*, book 2 (Washington, DC: Review and Herald®, 1958), 377.

3. Francis D. Nichol, ed., *The Seventh-day Adventist Bible Commentary*, vol. 7 (Hagerstown, MD: Review and Herald®, 1980), 678.

4. Ellen G. White, *Testimonies for the Church*, vol. 7 (Mountain View, CA: Pacific Press®, 1948), 21.

5. Ellen G. White, *Manuscript Releases*, vol. 9 (Silver Spring, MD: Ellen G. White Estate, 1990), 303.

6. Ellen G. White, *Our High Calling* (Washington, DC: Review and Herald®, 1961), 130.

Five

Spirit-Empowered Witnessing

His name was Nicodemus. He was a Jewish Pharisee and a member of the Sanhedrin, an elite council of the Jews. He was a tithe-paying, health-reforming, Sabbath-keeping, religious aristocrat, but there was something missing deep inside. There was a longing that all his religiosity could not satisfy. There was an aching longing in his soul. The Holy Spirit convicted him that maybe, just maybe, this itinerant preacher, Jesus of Nazareth, had the answers he so desperately wanted. John's Gospel introduces us to the story in these words: "This man came to Jesus by night" (John 3:2). He came by night because he wanted a private audience with Jesus.

We should not condemn Nicodemus because he came by night. Given his Orthodox Jewish background, it is a miracle that he came at all. Jesus immediately sensed Nicodemus's heart longing, and He carefully explained the process of new birth, making this striking statement: "The wind blows where it wishes, and you hear the sound of it, but cannot tell where it comes from and where it goes. So is everyone who is born of the Spirit" (verse 8). Here Christ reveals that the agency in the new birth is the Holy Spirit. It is the Holy Spirit who convicts us of sin. It is the Holy Spirit who draws our hearts to Jesus. It is the Holy Spirit who impresses truth upon our minds, and it is the Holy Spirit who changes our lives. Just as the invisible wind has highly visible effects, so the Holy Spirit has a dramatic impact on human lives.

Cooperation with the Holy Spirit

Our success in winning others to Christ depends on our cooperation with the Holy Spirit. Before we ever speak to an individual about Christ or before we witness to them in any way, the Holy Spirit already impresses their minds with the things of eternity. We cooperate with Christ in witnessing to lost people as we unite with and are empowered by the Holy Spirit. Without the empowerment and guidance of the Holy Spirit, our witnessing efforts are powerless. We may be able to convince someone of certain Bible truths, but without the deep working of the Holy Spirit in their lives, little change will take place. They may change their beliefs but not their hearts. There may be external conformity to truth, but there will be no life-changing transformation into the likeness of Christ.

In this chapter, we will study the role of the Holy Spirit in witnessing and His mighty power to change lives. Our study will consider specific examples recorded in the book of Acts that reveal the remarkable work of the Holy Spirit in the lives of unbelievers. These unbelievers came from various cultural backgrounds. Their life experiences were different. Some were educated, and others were uneducated. Some were wealthy, and others were poverty-stricken. Some were Jews, and others were Gentiles. They came from different continents and had different worldviews, yet all were impacted by the Holy Spirit. The Holy Spirit is no respecter of persons. He can transform any individual open to His influence. The primary purpose of this chapter is to reveal that as we cooperate with the Holy Spirit, we, too, will see His miracle-working power in the lives of those to whom we are witnessing. Before we delve into the power of the Holy Spirit in the book of Acts, it is necessary to review Jesus' teaching on the Holy Spirit in the Gospel of John.

Jesus' teaching on the Holy Spirit

Jesus' discourse in John chapters 14–16 is the New Testament's primary teaching on the ministry of the Holy Spirit. In the sixteenth chapter of John, Jesus made this remarkable statement to His disciples: "Nevertheless I tell you the truth. It is to your advantage that I go away; for if I do not go away, the Helper will not come to you; but if I depart, I will send Him to you" (John 16:7). The disciples must have been startled by Jesus' words. How could it be possible that it would be to their "advantage" if Jesus went away and left them alone on earth? Notice that Jesus does not call the Holy Spirit "it" but refers to the Holy Spirit as "Him." The Holy Spirit is the Third Person of the Godhead. Unlimited by time and space, He has all the power of divinity. Dwelling in human flesh, Jesus could be in only one place at one time, but the Holy Spirit could be present with each of the disciples in the fullness of divine power, wherever they journeyed in their witness for Christ.

The Holy Spirit is our Helper. The Greek word Jesus uses to describe Him is *paraclete*, which means "called to one's side."[1] The Holy Spirit is the one who comes alongside us to empower our witness, guide our words, and motivate our service for Christ. Witnessing is never about us. It is always about Jesus. The purpose of the Holy Spirit's ministry is to "testify" of Jesus. Our Lord clearly stated, "But when the Helper comes, whom I shall send to you from the Father, the Spirit of truth who proceeds from the Father, He will testify of Me. And you also will bear witness" (John 15:26, 27).

Note that the Holy Spirit bears witness and testifies, and we also bear witness. The Bible commentator Matthew Henry states, "The Spirit's working is not to supersede, but to engage and encourage ours."[2] Our work is to cooperate with the Holy Spirit in leading people to Jesus and His truth. It is the Holy Spirit's work to convince and convert. It is the Holy Spirit's work to reveal truth and righteousness. It is the Holy Spirit's work to place within the heart a desire to do right and the power to choose right.

A church-growth explosion in Acts

When Jesus told His disciples that the power of the Holy Spirit would come upon them and they would be witnesses to Him to the ends of the earth (Acts 1:8), they must have wondered how this could ever be possible. How could this little band of believers impact the world? How could they possibly fulfill Christ's command to "Go into all the world and preach the gospel to every creature" (Mark 16:15)? They were a small, mostly uneducated, insignificant band of believers. They had little means and a huge task—some would say an impossible task. Yet they understood that through the ministry of the Holy Spirit in God's power, nothing would be impossible (see Matthew 19:26).

But the early believers prayed. They sought God. They confessed their sins. They repented of their selfish attitudes. Barriers were broken down, and the believers were drawn closer to God and one another. During the ten days in the upper room, their lives were changed. They were now ready for the outpouring of the Holy Spirit.

As promised, God poured out His Spirit in an abundant measure at Pentecost. Three thousand were converted in a day. Acts 4 records that the number who believed were about five thousand men (Acts 4:4). If you count the women and children who were likely part of the crowd, the number who believed swells to somewhere between fifteen thousand and twenty thousand. In a short time, the growth of the New Testament church exploded.

In verses 31–33, we catch a brief glimpse of the continuing spiritual experience of the early believers and the ministry of the church. "And when they had prayed, the place where they were assembled together was shaken; and they were all filled with the Holy Spirit, and they spoke the word of God with boldness" (verse 31). Notice three facts here: They prayed. They earnestly sought God on their knees. They were filled with the Holy Spirit. Power from above flooded into their lives, and emerging from the crucible of prayer, they spoke the Word of God with confidence. Verse 33 adds, "And with great power the apostles gave witness to the resurrection of the Lord Jesus. And great grace was upon them all." The Greek verb translated "gave" in this passage is *apodidomi*, which can be translated "to deliver that which is due."[3]

Redeemed by His grace and transformed by His love, the disciples felt an inner compulsion to share their faith. They could not keep silent. They delivered the message that the world needed. They were debtors to the cross of Christ. The apostle Paul states it eloquently: "I am a debtor both to Greeks and to barbarians, both to wise and to unwise. So, as much as is in me, I am ready to preach the gospel" (Romans 1:14, 15). When our lives are transformed by the grace of God, the Holy Spirit convicts us of our need to share the marvels of His grace and the glory of His truth with others. The New Testament church flourished because the first-century believers could not keep silent about their relationship with Christ. As the apostle Paul stated, "For the love of Christ compels us" (2 Corinthians 5:14). The love of Christ filled their hearts and overflowed to all those around. The Holy Spirit transformed their lives, empowered their witness, and changed the world.

Commenting on Acts 4:33, the *Seventh-day Adventist Bible Commentary* states, "The witness of the apostles was presented, not in their own strength, but by a power they never could have engendered within themselves. Theirs was the energizing of the Divine Spirit."[4] It is the Holy Spirit who always empowers genuine, authentic witness and makes it efficient in the hearts of unbelievers. The witness of the New Testament believers bridged cultural barriers. It compelled them to cross continents. It led them into cities and villages, across barren deserts, through stormy seas, and up steep mountain pathways.

Filled with the Holy Spirit, these New Testament believers planted churches (Acts 9:31), broke social mores and cultural customs (Acts 10–15), and spread the gospel message throughout the Mediterranean world. The Holy Spirit led them on a remarkable journey of faith that resulted in tens of thousands accepting Jesus.

Commenting on the ministry of the Holy Spirit in the New

Testament church, Ellen White puts it this way:

> The Spirit came upon the waiting, praying disciples with a fullness that reached every heart. The Infinite One revealed Himself in power to His church. It was as if for ages this influence had been held in restraint, and now Heaven rejoiced in being able to pour out upon the church the riches of the Spirit's grace. And under the influence of the Spirit, words of penitence and confession mingled with songs of praise for sins forgiven. Words of thanksgiving and of prophecy were heard. All heaven bent low to behold and to adore the wisdom of matchless, incomprehensible love. Lost in wonder, the apostles exclaimed, "Herein is love." They grasped the imparted gift. And what followed? The sword of the Spirit, newly edged with power and bathed in the lightnings of heaven, cut its way through unbelief. Thousands were converted in a day.[5]

The Holy Spirit opens and shuts doors

There are times when the Holy Spirit shuts one door only to open another. The Holy Spirit's providence is illustrated in the life of the apostle Paul. On his second missionary journey, he was "forbidden by the Holy Spirit to preach the word in Asia" (Acts 16:6).

Perplexed and wondering where God was leading, Paul and his evangelistic team traveled through Asia and determined to preach the gospel in Bithynia, but "the Spirit did not permit them" (verse 7). Paul's motive was only to serve Christ and preach the gospel, but, on every hand, doors were shut in his face. Then in a vision, "a man of Macedonia stood and pleaded with him saying, 'Come over to Macedonia and help us' " (verse 9). At that time, God shut the door to specific geographical regions in Asia because the door of an entire continent was open to the gospel. When the Holy Spirit closes one door, He opens another.

God is the God of the open door. One of the functions of

the Holy Spirit is to open hearts to the gospel. He convicts the world of sin, righteousness, and judgment. The same Holy Spirit who opened the heart of Lydia; a slave girl; the Roman jailer; a Roman judge; Dionysius; and Crispus, the ruler of a Jewish synagogue, is still opening hearts and minds to the gospel today. The same Holy Spirit who prepared a Roman retirement community, Philippi, for Paul's witness is preparing communities today. The same Holy Spirit who went before Paul to Thessalonica, a blue-collar working community, has gone before us to prepare the way for major public evangelistic meetings in our cities today. The same Holy Spirit who worked in sophisticated Athens and decadent Corinth is still working in the cities of our world to create receptivity to the gospel. The same Holy Spirit who worked in ages past longs to empower your witness for Christ. He is waiting to fill our churches with the power of the Almighty to witness in their communities. Ellen White clearly states, "The promise of the Holy Spirit is not limited to any age or to any race. Christ declared that the divine influence of His Spirit was to be with His followers unto the end. From the Day of Pentecost to the present time, the Comforter has been sent to all who have yielded themselves fully to the Lord and to His service. To all who have accepted Christ as a personal Saviour, the Holy Spirit has come as a counselor, sanctifier, guide, and witness."[6]

The promise of the Holy Spirit is ours today. There is still power in the Word of God to transform lives by the power of the Holy Spirit. According to the apostle Peter, the Bible was written as "holy men of God spoke as they were moved by the Holy Spirit" (2 Peter 1:21). The same Holy Spirit who inspired the Bible works through the Word of God to change minds and transform lives as we share the Word. The power of New Testament witnessing was the power of the Holy Spirit through the Word of God to change lives. The apostles shared the Word. They were students of the Word, and their devotion to it allowed the Holy Spirit to work through them with great power.

Stay connected to God's power

The story is told of a couple that ordered a new refrigerator. Everything seemed to be working fine as the delivery man set up their new appliance. They filled their fridge with food and then left the house for a two-week vacation. When they returned home and opened the refrigerator door, they were greeted with a horrible smell. The milk had soured. The fruit and vegetables had spoiled. Something had gone wrong. It wasn't long before they discovered that there had been a power outage while they were away. The lack of power had spoiled the food, and it had to be thrown out.

Likewise, when the power of the Holy Spirit no longer flows through our lives, our witness becomes ineffective; it spoils. We cannot encourage the fruits of the Holy Spirit in the lives of unbelievers if the fruits of the Spirit are not manifest in our own lives. If we are "unplugged" from God, we are powerless. Jesus invites each one of us to open our hearts to the infilling of the Holy Spirit. It is this infilling that will give power to our witness. Without it, the church's programs and advertising will be ineffective. All the money in the world will produce no lasting results unless the Holy Spirit is available in all the fullness of divine power.

Carefully consider this promise: "The lapse of time has wrought no change in Christ's parting promise to send the Holy Spirit as His representative. It is not because of any restriction on the part of God that the riches of His grace do not flow earthward to men. If the fulfillment of the promise is not seen as it might be, it is because the promise is not appreciated as it should be. If all were willing, all would be filled with the Spirit."[7]

There are three simple steps to receive the Holy Spirit in His fullness: ask for the Holy Spirit (Luke 11:13; Zechariah 10:1), repent of any known sin (Acts 2:38; 3:19), and be willing to do whatever Christ asks you to do (Acts 5:32; John 14:15, 16). When you have fulfilled these conditions, God will honor His Word and pour out His Spirit on your life.

Prayerfully reflect on the following questions:

1. Are you connected to the Source of all power? What does it mean to be filled with the Holy Spirit?
2. Is there any barrier between you and someone else that would hinder your effectiveness in witness?
3. Have you ever attempted to witness in your own strength rather than in the power of the Holy Spirit?
4. What is your attitude toward witnessing? Do you believe that the Holy Spirit is opening doors of opportunity in your community? Is He regularly opening doors of opportunity for you in the lives of the people you meet every day?
5. Who are the specific people in your sphere of influence? Silently pray for opportunities to share God's love and truth with them.

1. "Paraclete," BibleStudyTools.com, accessed December 13, 2019, https://www.biblestudytools.com/dictionary/paraclete/

2. Matthew Henry, *Matthew Henry Bible Commentary on the Whole Bible*, Volume V-III-John, ed. Anthony Uyl (Woodstock, Ontario, Canada: Devoted Publishing, 2018), 282.

3. "Apodidomi," BibleStudyTools.com, accessed November 14, 2019, http://biblestudytools.com/lexicons/greek/nas/apodidomi.html.

4. Francis D. Nichol, ed., *The Seventh-day Adventist Bible Commentary*, vol. 6 (Washington, DC: Review and Herald®, 1957), 173.

5. Ellen G. White, *The Acts of the Apostles* (Mountain View, CA: Pacific Press®, 1911), 38.

6. White, *Acts of the Apostles*, 49.

7. White, *Acts of the Apostles*, 50.

Six

Unlimited Possibilities

It was one of those calls that stick in my memory. My pastor friend on the other end of the line was troubled. For months, he had attempted to move his church into a mission mode to reach their community for Christ. He preached sermons on the importance of witnessing and encouraged his members to be actively involved in soul-winning ministries in the community. As the capstone of this soul-winning emphasis, he climaxed his witnessing sermon series by inviting a specialist about spiritual gifts to conduct a weekend workshop. Anticipation was high. The weekend series was well attended. The members responded positively to the spiritual gifts test. As he described his efforts to me, I wondered why he was so concerned. Then he made this comment: "We have discovered that the members of my small congregation have 26 spiritual gifts, but I have no idea what to do now. Can you help me? Where do I go from here? I am quite frustrated in knowing how to proceed." My pastor friend is not alone.

Many Christians have practical questions about the gifts of the Spirit. What are spiritual gifts? Are they reserved for just a few super-Christians? Are they for every believer? How do I discover my spiritual gifts? What is the purpose of spiritual gifts? Once I discover my gifts, how can I use them in service for Christ? In this chapter, we will explore answers to these questions and make practical suggestions that can make a significant difference in your life.

What are spiritual gifts?

Spiritual gifts are intimately linked to the ministry of the Holy Spirit. The reason Scripture calls them *spiritual gifts* is because they are gifts, abilities, or talents imparted by the Holy Spirit to each believer for the glory of God. They are not to be used in selfish exhibitionism to show how talented we are or to draw attention to ourselves. Rightly understood, all the gifts imparted by the Holy Spirit are given for two essential purposes: to nurture or strengthen the body of Christ and to fulfill the mission of Christ in reaching the world with the gospel. Spiritual gifts are service gifts. They are gifts to bless the community of believers and the broader world community.

Each believer receives spiritual gifts, and these gifts have different functions. In Christ, everyone has equal value, but we do not have the same roles or the same gifts. This diversity of gifts strengthens the church and empowers its witness to the world. These differences are a strength and not a weakness. The Holy Spirit chooses what gifts to impart to each believer based on their background, culture, and personality. The Holy Spirit bestows gifts that will bring satisfaction in Christ's service and the greatest blessing to the church and the world.

The apostle Paul begins 1 Corinthians 12 with these words: "Now concerning spiritual gifts, brethren, I do not want you to be ignorant" (verse 1). The reason the apostle Paul spends the entire chapter of 1 Corinthians 12, most of Romans 12, and a large portion of Ephesians 4 on the topic of spiritual gifts is because a proper understanding of spiritual gifts is vital for both the nurture and the growth of the church. Spiritual gifts are at the very heart of effective soul winning. They are the foundation of a witnessing church.

Let's first answer some basic questions regarding spiritual gifts: What are spiritual gifts? How do they differ from natural talents? Who receives spiritual gifts? What is their purpose, and why are they given?

Spiritual gifts are divinely bestowed qualities given by the Holy Spirit to build the body of Christ and enable believers to be effective witnesses in the world. Spiritual gifts are the channel through which our ministry for Christ flows. Unbelievers may have many natural talents, but they are not used for the upbuilding of Christ's kingdom. They are often used to benefit one's self.

Of course, all of our abilities, whether we are believers or unbelievers, come from God. Every talent we have is God-given. Spiritual gifts differ from natural talents in two distinct ways: first, in the way they are used, and second, where they are used. The motivation for using natural abilities may be self-glory. The motivation for using spiritual gifts is always God's glory. Natural talents are often used to advance one's standing in the world. Spiritual gifts are unselfishly used to bless and expand God's church. The significant difference between spiritual gifts and natural talents is their focus. Natural talents may bring attention to the individual possessing them. Spiritual gifts are given by the Holy Spirit to bring glory to God.

Spiritual gifts are promised to each one who commits his or her life to Christ. Discussing spiritual gifts, the apostle Paul states, "But one and the same Spirit works all these things, distributing to each one individually as He wills" (1 Corinthians 12:11).

When we commit our lives to Jesus, the Holy Spirit imparts gifts for witnessing and service. Unconverted people may have natural talents in some specific areas of their lives. When they are converted, the Holy Spirit often redirects or repurposes those natural talents for the glory of God and the advancement of the cause of Christ. There are also times that the Holy Spirit imparts gifts that an individual never had before or imagined they could ever have. They now find fulfillment in using their newly discovered gifts for the service of Christ. As part of the body of Christ, they find joy in making their contribution to upbuilding Christ's church and participating in His mission.

According to our passage in 1 Corinthians 12:11, the Holy Spirit distributes spiritual gifts to "each one individually as He wills." The Holy Spirit does not impart the same gift to everyone, but He does give gifts to each believer. He does not overlook one individual. Each believer shares in the gifts of the Spirit. Ellen White underscores this vital truth. "To every person is committed some peculiar gift or talent which is to be used to advance the Redeemer's kingdom."[1]

I think of my mother. My father had the gift of teaching. He was an excellent Bible student, outgoing, witty, and a natural-born teacher, but Mom was a person that you hardly knew was present until she wasn't. Mom would feel uncomfortable if someone asked her to read the Scripture reading in church, and certainly, teaching Sabbath School was out of her league. When my mother became a Seventh-day Adventist, God gave her the gift of encouragement. She sought out people who sat on the sidelines and encouraged them. She listened sensitively to people's needs and met them as she was able. She had this uncanny sense to pick out the people who needed that extra boost and encourage them accordingly. The Holy Spirit divinely endowed her with this gift of encouragement.

Like my mother, each member has been given unique spiritual gifts through the ministry of the Holy Spirit. If we believe God's Word, we can thank God for the gifts He has given us and pray that He will reveal them to us, all for His glory. The Holy Spirit does not give gifts to a select few and neglect or bypass others who may seem less talented. The Holy Spirit imparts God's gifts to each one individually as He wills.

The Holy Spirit chooses the gifts

Let's suppose it's a friend's birthday. Who selects the birthday gift you will give? You will, of course. I remember, as a boy, I would make my birthday list, but my parents would ultimately be the ones who chose my gift. Most of the time, the choice they made was far better than the choice I would have made. They knew better than I did what would make me happy.

The Holy Spirit knows what gifts to impart to each believer

to best glorify Jesus in their lives. The *Seventh-day Adventist Bible Commentary* says, "The Holy Spirit delivers His gifts to believers in accordance with His knowledge of their capacities and the needs existing in the experience of each individual. It is not an arbitrary division, but one based on supreme knowledge and understanding."[2] This assurance should be a great source of encouragement to each one of us. We have the absolute assurance that the Holy Spirit has imparted the exact gifts we need to become effective witnesses for Christ. The gifts you have are the ones that the Holy Spirit has deemed needful for your spiritual growth and the cause of Christ.

Varied gifts best contribute to Christ's body

Although the church is one body, it is composed of a variety of members, all contributing to the goal of revealing Christ to the world. Writing to the members of the church at Rome, the apostle Paul states, "So we, being many, are one body in Christ, and individually members of one another. Having then gifts according to the grace that is given to us, let us use them" (Romans 12:5, 6). The apostle amplifies this thought in 1 Corinthians 12:12: "For as the body is one and has many members, but all the members of that one body, being many, are one body, so also is Christ."

In human beings, each body part has a function. There are no inactive members of the body. Each one has been placed in the body to play a specific role. Each one has a unique function. Each member of the human body contributes to the overall well-being of the entire body. In the same way, the church needs active members who are committed to contributing to the overall health of the church, the body of Christ.

In 1 Corinthians 12, Romans 12, and Ephesians 4, the Bible gives us examples of some of the gifts God places in His church. Some of those gifts are leadership gifts, such as apostles, prophets, evangelists, pastors, and teachers. The purpose of these leadership gifts is to facilitate unity, foster spiritual growth, and equip church members for mission. These same passages also speak of gifts that are ministry gifts given to each believer. A few examples are hospitality, liberality, helps, mercy, and healing.

Many of these gifts are qualities of a converted heart. Each one of us should exhibit hospitality to others in our daily walk with Christ. Each believer is called to be liberal in their giving patterns. Each Christian should help and support others. We are to seek ways to bless and minister God's healing grace to all those around us. If these qualities are the natural response of the converted heart, why are they considered spiritual gifts selected by the Holy Spirit for some and not others?

The answer is simply this: While each believer is called to reveal a gracious, hospitable spirit in their lives, every believer is not called to the special ministry of hospitality. While we are all called to be liberal, we are not all called to a ministry in which liberality becomes our means of service for Christ. Conversion brings changes in our lives. We long to reveal the qualities of a Christlike life daily. The Holy Spirit amplifies and expands those qualities, and as He does, some of these qualities become our channel of service in Christ's church. At times, He imparts new qualities as spiritual gifts, helping us to discover our most satisfying and productive role in the body of Christ. As the apostle Paul states, this creates an "effective working by which every part does its share" and "causes growth of the body, for the edifying of itself in love" (Ephesians 4:16).

If the Holy Spirit imparts spiritual gifts to all believers for the upbuilding of God's church and its witness in the world, how can we discover our spiritual gifts? Here are some simple steps that will help you discover your spiritual gifts.

First, ask God to reveal the gifts He has imparted to you. Scripture says, "Every good gift and every perfect gift is from above, and comes down from the Father of lights, with whom there is no variation or shadow of turning" (James 1:17). The God who imparts His precious gifts to each one of us will also reveal them through His Holy Spirit (see Luke 11:13).

Second, seek the advice of respected spiritual leaders. Tell them how God is leading in your life, and ask about areas of service that might be available.

And finally, begin using your gifts to help the body of Christ.

The purpose of God's gifts is service. As you start using the gifts He has given you, they will expand, and your abilities will increase. Spiritual gifts do not arrive fully developed; they become more effective as you use them. Ellen White powerfully describes this process: "He who will give himself fully to God will be guided by the divine hand. He may be lowly and apparently ungifted; yet if with a loving, trusting heart he obeys every intimation of God's will, his powers will be purified, ennobled, energized, and his capacities will be increased."[3]

As we use the gifts God has given us, we will find joy and satisfaction. Others will confirm our giftedness in a particular area, and the church will be blessed. Remember, spiritual gifts do not come fully developed. The Holy Spirit imparts gifts and blesses them when they are put to use.

Here is a practical example. I had no idea that I might have the gift of "preaching" or "proclamation." As a college theology student, I was extremely nervous in any public speaking appointment. Often, I lost my place in my notes and felt embarrassed after my presentation. But something remarkable happened. As I continued to preach, my confidence level grew. The gift that God had given me flourished. I know that it was much more than spending hours studying for my sermons. It was much more than practicing my delivery. It was much more than gaining more experience. Although these things were necessary, the most important realization was that I had been gifted by God, and He was delivering on His promise to equip me for ministry.

Ellen White gives us this divine assurance: "God calls upon His people, many of whom are but half awake, to arouse, and engage in earnest labor, praying for strength for service. Workers are needed. Receive the Holy Spirit, and your efforts will be successful. Christ's presence is what gives power."[4] As we use the gifts God has given us, they grow. Someone has rightly said, "If you do not use it, you will lose it." The corollary is, "As we go, we will grow." As we go to work for Christ, we will grow in our ability to do His work. Christianity is not a spectator sport. We are called to service. The God that calls us to His service equips us for that service. The Holy Spirit does not call the qualified; He qualifies the called. //

Throughout the book of Acts, the Holy Spirit guides, directs, teaches, and strengthens believers in their witness to the world. God is not looking for supersmart or super-talented people; He is looking for super-consecrated people. People who are entirely dependent on the Holy Spirit. People who recognize that without the power of the Spirit, their witness is powerless. God does not look for ability. He looks for availability. His Word is clear: "Not by might nor by power, but by My Spirit says, the Lord" (Zechariah 4:6). The Holy Spirit is essential for effective witnessing. He prepares people for the proclamation of the gospel, causing hearts and minds to be receptive to the influence of God's Word. The Holy Spirit imparts spiritual gifts to each believer and enables each one to develop those gifts as he or she uses them in service. In this way, a lasting impact is made in the lives of others. //

More than anything else, God is looking for men and women, boys and girls, youth, and young adults who are fully, completely committed to sharing His love with a lost world. Their hearts are knit with His heart, and each mind is one with His mind. Their greatest desire is to share His love so that people can receive the gift of eternal life. They are committed to using their gifts for the advancement of God's cause. /

On your knees, seeking God, have you asked Him to impress you with the gifts He has given you? Have you opened your heart to the living Christ and asked Him to reveal your place of service? Are you willing to pray this simple prayer? //

"Dear Lord, I acknowledge that without the gifts and power of the Holy Spirit, my witness is powerless. I thank You that You have promised gifts to every believer, and I commit myself to use the gifts You have given me in service to Your church and the people around me. I humbly ask that You reveal the place You would like me to serve and empower me to use my gifts under the direction of the Holy Spirit. Thank You for the gifts of the Spirit and Your guidance in using them effectively in Your cause. In Jesus' name, amen." //

Unlimited Possibilities

1. Ellen G. White, *Testimonies for the Church*, vol. 4 (Mountain View, CA: Pacific Press®, 1948), 618.

2. Francis D. Nichol, *Seventh-day Adventist Bible Commentary*, vol. 6 (Hagerstown, MD: Review and Herald®, 1980), 772.

3. Ellen G. White, *Acts of the Apostles* (Mountain View, CA: Pacific Press®, 1911), 283.

4. Ellen G. White, "Power for Service," *The Central Advance*, February 25, 1903.

Seven

Sharing the Word

Buck was a rough-and-tumble gang member in a large city in northeastern America. He often spent Saturday nights bar-hopping, drinking, and picking fights for entertainment. It was not unusual for him to break a beer bottle over a bar and engage someone from another gang in a bottle fight. His goal was to cut them up before they could cut him. Buck was tough, really tough. But his six-foot-plus frame, bulging muscles, and fearless appearance only masked an aching longing to find real purpose and peace in his life.

One day, an Adventist friend invited him to one of our evangelistic meetings. As he rode up to the meetings on his Harley-Davidson motorcycle with his black leather jacket, worn jeans, and motorcycle boots, he did not appear to have any spiritual interest. But there was something about Buck that went beyond his appearance. It was his eyes. They seemed to signal a hunger for something more.

Buck was looking for something to satisfy his heart's longing, and night after night, he eagerly listened to the Word of God being powerfully proclaimed. His heart was touched. His life was changed. The Christ of the Word became his personal Savior. The prophecies of Scripture gave him new confidence in a God who guides the future. The teachings of the Bible changed his life. The Holy Spirit transformed him from an angry gang member to a grace-filled, loving Christian believer.

The power of the Word

The inspired Word of God contains life-giving principles. When we accept the Christ-centered teachings of Scripture by faith, our lives are transformed. The creative power of the Word of God illuminates our darkness. It changes us. When God spoke the Word at Creation, our planet came into existence. He created this world by His all-powerful Word. The psalmist states,

> By the word of the LORD were the heavens made,
> And all the host of them by the breath of His mouth. . . .
> For He spoke, and it was done;
> He commanded, and it stood fast (Psalm 33:6, 9).

God's Word is a creative Word. What He says is so because His Word is so powerful; it creates what it declares. The audible Word, proceeding out of God's mouth, creates tangible matter. You and I can declare what is, but only God can declare what is not, and what is not appears. When God speaks, His Word makes it so. Speaking about Abraham and Sarah's conception in old age, Paul states this remarkable truth: "God . . . calls those things which do not exist as though they did" (Romans 4:17). Before Sarah ever conceived a child, God's Word declared that she would become pregnant in old age. This divine pronouncement became a reality because God's Word has the power to accomplish what God declares.

Here is a marvelous, life-changing truth: the creative power of the spoken Word is in the written Word. The apostle Paul declared, "For the word of God is living and powerful, and sharper than any two-edged sword, piercing even to the division of soul and spirit, and of joints and marrow, and is a discerner of the thoughts and intents of the heart" (Hebrews 4:12). The Bible is the living Word of God. Through the ministry of the Holy Spirit, it becomes alive in our hearts and changes our lives.

Other books may be inspiring, but God's Word is inspired. Other books may enlighten the mind, but God's Word not only enlightens us—it also transforms us. Ellen White captures the awesome power of God's Word in this statement: "The creative energy that called the worlds into existence is in the word of God. This word imparts power; it begets life. Every command is a promise; accepted by the will, received into the soul, it brings with it the life of the Infinite One. It transforms the nature and re-creates the soul in the image of God."[1] Think about this statement for a moment. When we share the Word of God with others, Creation takes place all over again. The power of the Word brings light into darkened minds. The power of the Word quenches thirsty souls and feeds hungry hearts. It re-creates the soul in the image of God.

Jesus: The Living Word

The central theme of the Bible is Jesus. The prophets of the Old Testament testified of Him. Each book of the Bible is a revelation of His love. Speaking to the Pharisees, Jesus declared, "You search the Scriptures, for in them you think you have eternal life; and these are they which testify of Me" (John 5:39). The Old Testament speaks of the Christ who will come, and the New Testament reveals the Christ who has come. The entire Bible "testifies" of Jesus. In Scripture, Jesus is the dying Lamb, the living Priest, and the coming King. He is the one who justifies us, sanctifies us, and, one day, will glorify us. Jesus is our forgiving, merciful, compassionate, life-changing Savior and Lord. Jesus is the great miracle worker. He is a life changer. "If anyone is in Christ, he is a new creation; old things have passed away; behold, all things have become new" (2 Corinthians 5:17).

The Bible is not merely a how-to manual on the Christian life; it is the living Word of God that transforms lives. Consider some of the scriptural symbols of the Word, such as light, fire, a hammer, seed, and bread. These different images have one thing in common: they reveal the power of God's Word to change our lives. When you share the Word of God with the people in your sphere of influence, it is like a light that guides them through the dark valleys of their lives. It is like a fire that burns within their soul. It is like a hammer that breaks their hard hearts. It is like seed that silently grows and produces the fruit of the Spirit in their lives. It is like bread that nourishes their spiritual hunger.

Symbols of God's Word

The psalmist David declares, "Your Word is a lamp to my feet and a light to my path" (Psalm 119:105). He also adds, "The entrance of Your words gives light; it gives understanding to the simple" (verse 130). Light always involves the removal of darkness. If you were on a dark path at night without a light, you might quickly drift off the path. A powerful flashlight would make all the difference in the world.

In the same way, the Word of God lights the pathway of the followers of Christ. It guides them home. Jesus is the "light of the world" (John 8:12), who lights up our darkness through His Word. When we share the Word of God with others, it dispels the darkness enshrouding their lives and lights their pathway to the kingdom of God.

My wife and I live about a mile from our Living Hope Seventh-day Adventist Church. Often, after an evening program, we will walk home. Our journey home takes us along an unlit path through the woods. We have walked that path in almost total darkness at times, and it is challenging to keep on the path and find our way. We have learned by experience that having a flashlight makes all the difference. When the light illumines the path, the walk home is quite pleasant. Without the light, we are groping in the darkness. Jesus longs to get us home, so He has provided His Word as a lamp to light the way.

Jeremiah 23:23 compares God's Word to both a fire and a hammer. It is compared to a fire because it consumes. When we share the Word of God with others, the fire of God's Word burns within their soul, consuming error. Like gold refined in the fire, the dross is consumed. The refining process is not

65

always pleasant, but it is necessary to remove the dross in their characters. God's Word is also like a hammer. The term *hammer* may seem like a rare term to use to describe the Bible. Hammers nail things together. They also smash things. The hammer of God's Word breaks hard hearts into pieces. Think of the dramatic changes that took place in the lives of the demoniacs, the Roman centurion, the thief on the cross, and a host of others throughout the New Testament. The Word of God pounded away at their hard hearts until they were broken by the hammer of love.

In one of the more common symbols in Scripture, the Bible is compared to seed. In Luke 8:11, Jesus states, "The seed is the word of God." There is life in a tiny seed. When the seed of God's Word is planted in the soil of the mind, it produces an abundant harvest in the life. Jesus often used the symbolism of seed to describe the growth of His kingdom. The Word of God scattered like seed throughout the world will produce a bountiful harvest. Jesus expands on this theme in one of His farming parables. "And He said, 'The kingdom of God is as if a man should scatter seed on the ground, and should sleep by night and rise by day, and the seed should sprout and grow, he himself does not know how' " (Mark 4:26, 27). Bible commentator Matthew Henry, commenting on this passage, makes this insightful statement: "It [the seed] will *come up*; though it seem lost and buried under the clods, it will find or make its way through them. The seed *cast into the ground will spring* [forth]. Let but the word of Christ have the place it ought to have in a soul, and it will show itself, as the *wisdom from above* doth in a *good conversation*."[2] Dr. Henry's point is clear. The Word of God may seem buried somewhere within the mind, covered under the clods of sin, but if it is cherished, it will spring forth into new life. It will radically change our attitude, our conversation, and our lifestyle. A seed is life-giving. We may not see the seed growing, but it is growing beneath the soil. As we sow the seed of the Word of God in the lives of people in our sphere of influence, it may appear that very little is happening in their lives. Sometimes it may even appear that the seed is wasted, but did you notice Jesus' statement? Here is the Master's point. We sow the seed, and God grows the seed. Our responsibility is not to grow seed; it is to sow seed.

The Bible also uses the term *bread* to describe the Word of God. Jesus said, "I am the bread of life" (John 6:35). He adds, "Man shall not live by bread alone, but by every word that proceeds from the mouth of God" (Matthew 4:4). Bread is the staff of life throughout the ancient world and one of our planet's basic foods. It is an essential dietary item. An individual can survive a long time on only bread and water. By using the illustration of bread, Jesus is declaring that He is essential for life.

Following the miracle of the feeding of the five thousand, in His well-known bread of life sermon, Jesus declares, "Whoever eats My flesh and drinks My blood has eternal life" (John 6:54). This seems like a strange statement. What could Jesus possibly be talking about? He was not talking about literally eating His flesh and drinking His blood. By feasting on His Word, His teachings become a very part of our lives. Being nourished by the Word is what Jeremiah meant when he joyfully declared,

> Your words were found, and I ate them,
> And Your word was to me the joy and rejoicing of my
>   heart;
> For I am called by Your name,
> O Lord God of hosts (Jeremiah 15:16).

The Word of God, like a piece of whole wheat bread, satisfies our hidden hunger. Have you ever noticed that highly refined products are neither satisfying nor filling? The Word of God is the staff of life. It nourishes our souls. And of course, the Scriptures are like a cold draft of pure refreshing water. They completely satisfy. There is nothing as rewarding as the discovery of the truth about Jesus in every teaching of Scripture. When we share the beautiful truths of Jesus and the encouraging promises of His Word, others around us are blessed beyond measure.

Discerning receptivity in others

When people are going through a transition in their lives, they are more likely to be open to the gospel. They may be facing health challenges, a job crisis, a relationship issue, or some other difficulty in their lives. Ask God to help you be sensitive to people around you and give you the wisdom to discern their openness to the Word of God.

Jan had just moved to a new city. Her husband died, and she was becoming disillusioned with her faith. A Bible-study interest card arrived at her door. Although she may not have been interested in an in-depth study of God's Word a year or so before the card arrived, she was going through a transition in her life and looking for something more. She had a hidden hunger that could not be satisfied with a superficial faith. She responded to the mailing, sent in the Bible study interest card, and studied the Bible lessons. Today, she is rejoicing in the truth of God's Word.

As I have emphasized throughout this chapter, the fantastic thing about God's Word is that it carries with it the power to accomplish what it declares. God's Word is living. Other books may be inspiring, but the Bible is inspired and contains the power of the Life-Giver. It does not merely contain truth; it is truth in its very essence. The living truths of the Bible not only declare what is so but also accomplish what they declare in the lives of those who believe (see Hebrews 3:19; 4:12).

Scripture assures us that through the Word of God, we become "partakers of the divine nature" (2 Peter 1:4), save our souls through the "implanted word" (James 1:21), and receive "an inheritance among all those who are sanctified" (Acts 20:32). When by faith we accept the Word of God as the living Word of Christ, everything Jesus has promised us becomes ours. His Word is "profitable for doctrine, for reproof, for correction, for instruction in righteousness" (2 Timothy 3:16).

Our primary goal as we share the Word with others is to communicate an exalted view of the inspired Word of God and encourage them to share the promises and teachings of the Word with others. Our role is not to convert people; that is the

Holy Spirit's role. Our role is to share the life-changing teachings of God's Word and allow the Holy Spirit to impress these teachings on the lives of others.

The promises of God's Word are like a good credit card. At times when people go on vacation to a foreign country and do not want to risk taking cash, they carry a credit card that is issued by a bank. Their credit card is risk-free. If they lose it or it is stolen, it is backed up by the bank. God's promises are backed up by all the riches in glory. Heaven's exhaustless riches never run out. Best of all, their benefits have already been purchased for us on the cross. All we do is accept the provisions of His promises by faith, and even faith itself is a gift He gives us.

Here are some promises to fix in your mind:

- If we confess our sins, He is faithful and just to forgive us our sins and to cleanse us from all unrighteousness (1 John 1:9).

- No temptation has overtaken you except such as is common to man; but God is faithful, who will not allow you to be tempted beyond what you are able, but with the temptation will also make the way of escape, that you may be able to bear it (1 Corinthians 10:13).

- I can do all things through Christ who strengthens me (Philippians 4:13).

- And my God shall supply all your need according to His riches in glory by Christ Jesus (Philippians 4:19).

- Now this is the confidence that we have in Him, that if we ask anything according to His will, He hears us. And if we know that He hears us, whatever we ask, we know that we have the petitions that we have asked of Him (1 John 5:14, 15).

Write each of these promises on an index card, read them over each day, and memorize them. Ask God to help you share them with someone in need, someone whose heart is being drawn to Him.

Finally, be ready to share with one of your Christian friends how God has used you this week. For example, several years ago, I was counseling a woman who was struggling to give up smoking. She had started as a teenager. Now in her adult life, she appeared hopelessly addicted. She had little confidence she could quit. All her previous efforts left her only more discouraged. We studied the New Testament together, focusing mainly on the miraculous healings of Jesus. Eventually, I read 1 John 5:14. "Now this is the confidence that we have in Him, that if we ask anything according to His will, He hears us."

I asked Carol where this text says our confidence is. Is it in our willpower? Is it in ourselves? Is it in our strength? No, our trust is in Him. We find our strength in Jesus. I pointed out that our text does not say, "Now this is the confidence that we have in Him, if we ask anything according to His will except give up smoking, He hears us." She smiled. When I asked, "Is it God's will for you to give up smoking?" her response was, "Pastor, of course, it is." She grasped the promise of God by faith. Faithful to His word, Jesus delivered her. Yes, she had a struggle, but grace is greater than sin. Faith triumphed over doubt. The power of God filled her life, and she became tobacco-free.

There is power, life-changing power, in the Word of God. As you share the Word of God with others, you will experience the joy of seeing Creation all over again as the same Holy Spirit that inspired the Word transforms lives through the Word.

---

1. Ellen G. White, *Education* (Nampa, ID: Pacific Press®, 2002), 126.
2. Matthew Henry, *Matthew Henry's Commentary on the Whole Bible*, vol. 5, Matthew–John, http://www.ccel.org/ccel/henry/mhc5.Mark.v.html.

Eight

Ministering Like Jesus

Han Zicheng survived the Japanese invasion, the Chinese Civil War, and the Cultural Revolution, but he knew he could not endure the sorrow of living alone. On a chilly December day, the eighty-five-year-old Chinese grandfather gathered some scraps of white paper and wrote out a plea in blue ink, "Looking for someone to adopt me, a lonely old man in his eighties. Strong-bodied. Can shop, cook, and take care of himself. No chronic illness. I retired from a scientific research institute in Tianjin, with a pension of 6,000 RMB [$950] a month," he wrote. "I won't go to a nursing home. My hope is that a kindhearted person or family will adopt me, nourish me through old age, and bury my body when I'm dead."[1]

He taped a copy to a bus shelter in his busy neighborhood. A young woman saw the ad and took a picture of it with her phone. When she placed the picture on social media, it went viral. Han received multiple calls, but unfortunately, before he could be adopted, he died of brokenhearted loneliness. As I thought about Han's story, it occurred to me that millions of desperate people in our world are seeking a loving embrace. They long for a kind word, a note of encouragement, and the joy of knowing that someone cares.

Jesus models self-sacrificial love

Jesus' ministry of self-sacrificial love revealed the nature of the kingdom of God. His words made an impact because His self-less life was in harmony with His words. His teachings made an impact because His loving actions were the outgrowth of His teachings. If Christ's actions were not in harmony with His words, He would have had little real influence on the people around Him. The officers of the temple reported to the chief priests and Pharisees, "No man ever spoke like this Man!" (John 7:46). Commenting on this passage, Andrew Pink adds, "What a testimony was this from unbelievers! Instead of arresting Him, they had been arrested by what they had heard. Mark again how this magnifies Christ as 'the Word'! It was not His miracles which had so deeply impressed them, but His speech! 'Never man spake as this man.' True indeed was their witness, for the One they had listened to was more than 'man'—'the Word was God'! No man ever spake like Christ because His words were spirit and life (John 6:63)."[2] Jesus' words were backed up by His actions. Had He not lived as He lived, He could not have spoken as He spoke. This is certainly true when it comes to our Christian witness. Our words have power when they are supported by a godly life.

This chapter underscores the importance of self-sacrificing service that is focused on other people, service that makes a lasting impression in their lives. We will examine the outflowing of love from Jesus' heart as His most effective means of witness.

Love answers Satan's charges

Long ago, in the vast heavenly realms of space, Lucifer rebelled against God. He claimed that God was unfair, unjust, and unloving. However, Jesus came to earth, demonstrated His Father's immense love, and refuted Satan's claims. Every miracle of healing revealed the Father's love. Every time a demon-possessed individual was delivered, the occasion spoke of the Father's love. Every time Jesus fed the hungry, comforted the sorrowing, forgave the guilty, strengthened the weak, or raised the dead, the Father's love was revealed.

Today, the church is the body of Christ, meeting people's needs in Jesus' name, revealing His love, and ministering to the community. Through the church, a watching world and waiting universe see the gracious character of God. Just as Christ testified to the truthfulness of His words by His selfless actions, so He calls His church to move past pious platitudes and engage in service.

Christ calls us to engage the world, not distance ourselves from it. We are called to light the darkness with the light of Christ's love. Light overcomes the darkness. The apostle Paul states it beautifully. "For it is the God who commanded light to shine out of darkness who has shone in our hearts to give the light of the knowledge of the glory of God in the face of Jesus Christ" (2 Corinthians 4:6).

Did you catch the significance of Paul's teaching? The light of God's love shines out of our lives to those in darkness. Through us, the glory of God can reach the world with a knowledge of His loving character.

The Bible also uses the imagery of salt to illustrate the role of Christian witness in our world. Salt is not going to give food much flavor if it stays in the saltshaker. It is only as salt is added to food that it can both flavor and preserve it. A few years ago, I read Rebecca Manley Pippert's book titled *Out of the Saltshaker*. In it, she presents evangelism not as an event but as a way of life. The book's central theme is simple: if you are going to make an impact on the world around you, get involved in people's lives. Christians who remain together in the comfortable confines of their churches and have little contact with the world will have little opportunity to influence it for Christ.

I was teasing my wife the other day and said, "I am tempted to write a new book, titled, *Why I Am Leaving the Church*."

She immediately responded, "What are you possibly thinking?"

I replied, "Look, you can't win souls if you stay in the church building. You must interact with your community. I am leaving the church building to go out and witness in our world." If the church becomes a monastic order rather than a mission movement, it will miss its eternal destiny and fail to carry out Christ's divine commission.

A mission movement, not a monastic order

The monastic movement of the Middle Ages considered the world to be evil. The monks believed that the way to holiness was to abandon the things of this world. Some of them went to extreme lengths to avoid contact with the world.

In his attempt to achieve holiness and be separate from the world, Simeon Stylites dwelt atop a series of pillars for thirty-seven years in a small town outside of Aleppo, Syria. As an ascetic monk, he spent his days meditating, praying, and contemplating the divine. Often people gathered around the pillar where he stood. They gazed at this "holy man" and sometimes asked for his advice. His fame spread throughout the surrounding area, and other monks imitated his lifestyle. They believed that oneness with God is achieved through separation from the world.

While Scripture calls each of us to prayer, meditation on the Word, and separation from evil, the purpose of spending time with Christ is so that we can witness to others. The monastics often missed this vital aspect of the Christian faith. They failed to understand that the power of a Christian witness is most potent when believers connect with their community.

Jesus' great intercessory prayer in John 17 puts it this way: "I do not pray that You should take them out of the world, but that You should keep them from the evil one" (verse 15). Someone has said that Christians are like a boat in the water. It is all right for the boat to be in the water if there is no water in the boat. Christians are in the world to influence it for Christ, but when the world is in Christians, absorbing their time, attention, and energies, something is wrong.

Jesus plunged into this sinful, rebellious world to reveal the love of God and redeem humanity. He viewed each person through the eyes of divine compassion. To a Roman military officer, He said, "I have not found such great faith, not even in Israel!" (Matthew 8:10). Surprisingly, He encouraged a Jewish scribe by saying, "You are not far from the kingdom of God" (Mark 12:34). While the disciples may have wanted to debate with this scribe, Jesus chose to believe the best about him. He saw each person as a candidate for the kingdom of God.

Words of hope

According to Isaiah's prophecy, Jesus would not break a "bruised reed" or quench "smoking flax" (Isaiah 42:2, 3). In other words, Jesus gently healed bruised people. He did not further condemn them. Think of the stinging words of condemnation Jesus could have given to the woman caught in adultery or the Samaritan woman at the well. Think of the rebuke He could have given Simon Peter after his denial or the stern criticism He could have had for the thief on the cross. But Jesus did none of this. His words were words of hope. They were words of grace, mercy, and forgiveness. He gives us this admonition: "Let your speech always be with grace, seasoned with salt, that you may know how you ought to answer each one" (Colossians 4:6). As Ellen White states so clearly, "Only by love is love awakened."[3] She adds, "The wonderful love of Christ will melt and subdue hearts, when the mere reiteration of doctrines would accomplish nothing."[4] When loving words are combined with thoughtful actions that meet practical human needs, unconverted hearts are changed.

Meeting needs

Jesus' method of evangelism was to find a need and meet it. His comprehensive threefold ministry of preaching, teaching, and healing transformed lives. The Gospels reveal Jesus meeting the "felt" needs of people so that He could touch them at the point of their deepest spiritual needs. Felt needs are the needs a person perceives they have at a fixed moment in time. In addition to our felt needs, each one of us has deeply embedded eternal longings. The Holy Spirit places spiritual desires within our hearts. As we meet people's felt needs, their prejudice is broken down, relationships are formed, and we earn the right to be heard. Jesus met people's felt needs so that they were willing to listen to the eternal truths He shared.

Consider the Gospel of John. In John 1:37, two disciples met Jesus. He immediately asked them, "What are you seeking?" These four words became Jesus' modus operandi of ministry. He always met people where they were, never where He was. He started with their physical, mental, social, and spiritual needs, not His own. In John 2, at the wedding feast in Cana of Galilee, Jesus met a social need by saving the host from the embarrassment of running out of wine. In John 3, Jesus met Nicodemus's heart hunger for authentic faith. Formal religion did not satisfy the Pharisee's needs. Jesus sensed his inner longing and made a direct spiritual appeal. In John 4, Jesus treated the Samaritan woman with dignity and respect, meeting her emotional need for a sense of self-worth.

Although she was a woman of ill-repute who had had five husbands, Jesus saw beyond her immediate situation. He kindly spoke to her inmost longings. For the first time in her life, she sensed genuine love. In John 5, Jesus met physical needs in the miraculous healing of a desperately ill man who had lain hopelessly by the pool of Bethesda for thirty-eight years. The name *Bethesda* means "house of mercy." Every place Jesus went, He ministered mercy. Luke, the New Testament physician, quotes Peter as saying that "Jesus . . . went about doing good" (Acts 10:38). Too often, we just go about, but Jesus invites us to change our paradigm. Life is about much more than going about. It involves "going about doing good."

Another example of this is found in John 6, when Jesus broke bread and fed five thousand hungry people. Jesus was concerned for His listeners and met their felt needs. Not surprisingly, the crowd was wowed and wanted to make Him king (verses 14, 15).

What made Jesus' popularity so high at this point in His ministry? The world had never seen One with such unselfish love. It had never experienced One who could meet physical, mental, emotional, and spiritual needs. It is here in John 6 that Jesus preached the powerful sermon on the bread of life. For the first time, many of His hearers understood that He was calling them to deep spiritual commitment, a commitment that caused many to walk away, unwilling to surrender their lives to Jesus (verse 66).

Jesus' concern for the "felt needs" of people was good public relations for the Christian church. However, His mission was much more than that of a philanthropic organization. The purpose of Jesus' life was to "seek and save that which was lost" (Luke 19:10). After healing scores of people on a Saturday night, Jesus was up early the next morning, seeking the Father in prayer. Although there were still more sick people to heal, Jesus said, "Let us go into the next towns that I may preach there also, because for this purpose I have come forth [into the world]" (Mark 1:38).

There is nothing more important to Jesus than saving lost people. He did not relieve disease so that individuals would have more energy to live lives of selfish indulgence. He relieved physical suffering to reveal the Father's love and to provide tangible evidence of His ability to heal hearts. All of Jesus' physical miracles served to illustrate His divine power to deliver from the bondage of sin.

The man with the golden key

My wife and I enjoyed living in England from 1985 to 1990. Those were some of the happiest years of our lives. Traditionally, English families are extremely close. Evenings in those years were often spent helping the kids with their homework or playing simple games. One traditional game that English children enjoyed was a game of cardboard cutouts of a theater and music scene. There were many characters in the game, and the children could make their theater scene along with the orchestra, choirs, and actors.

Each game came with "the man with the golden key." The man with the golden key could unlock any door and had access to the solution to any problem. Jesus is like that. He is the Man with the golden key, providing solutions for our deepest needs and most significant problems. For Him, closed doors, locked rooms, and darkened chambers are no problem. His love is the golden key that changes lives. His love leads us from the confines of our claustrophobic self-interests to the irreplaceable joy of meeting the needs of others. Ellen White offers this compelling summary of Christ's ministry: "Christ's method alone will give true success in reaching the people. The Saviour mingled with men as one who desired their good. He showed His sympathy for them, ministered to their needs, and won their confidence. Then He bade them, 'Follow Me.' "[5]

Spend a few minutes thinking about someone in your sphere of influence who has a real need you might be able to meet. Maybe there is a single mom who needs a break from the kids. What can you do to give her a "mom's night out?" How can you befriend her? Can you invite her home for a meal? What about offering to change the oil in her car?

Is there a retired widower living across the street? He is lonely and needs friendship. What practical things can you do for him? What about the young couple who have just moved into the apartment down the hall from yours or into the house across the street? How can you help them become better acquainted with the community?

Think about the people in your sphere of influence who need better health. They may desire to quit smoking, adopt a healthier diet, lose weight, reduce stress, exercise more, or have a better lifestyle. How can your church develop an ongoing, comprehensive health outreach in its community? The service opportunities are endless, and the Holy Spirit will guide you in your efforts to relieve suffering humanity.

If we are eager to walk in the footsteps of Jesus, we should consider concrete ways to meet our communities' needs in His name. If we are going to be followers of Jesus, let's love as He loved, minister as He ministered, and serve as He served.

---

1. Emily Rauhala, "The Lonely Grandpa," *Winnipeg Free Press*, May 12, 2018, F11.

2. Andrew Pink, "Chapter—Christ in the Temple (Concluded)," Bible Explore .com, http://www.godrules.net/library/pink/NEWpink_a27.htm.

3. Ellen G. White, *The Desire of Ages* (Mountain View, CA: Pacific Press®, 1940), 22.

4. White, *Desire of Ages*, 826.

5. Ellen G. White, *The Ministry of Healing* (Mountain View, CA: Pacific Press®, 1942), 143.

Nine

Developing
a Winning Attitude

Children are our best teachers, and grandchildren are the best of all. When Dyson, our grandson, was in the second grade, he was standing in line waiting for the morning bell to ring, eager to go into his classroom. The little girl in front of him looked down at his new shoes, hesitated for a moment, and then said, "I think your shoes are ugly." Without giving it much thought, our grandson looked down at her shoes and commented, "I think your shoes are beautiful." Immediately her attitude changed. Kindness fosters kindness. The wise man was right; "a soft answer turns away wrath" (Proverbs 15:1).

Our attitude toward others often determines their response toward us. Have you ever noticed that when you smile at someone, they usually smile back? Have you also seen that when you respond with an unexpected compliment, other people generally respond positively? When you believe the best about others, it lifts their spirits and encourages their hearts.

Jesus understood this fact about human nature. John's Gospel states that Jesus "is the true Light which gives light to every man coming into the world" (John 1:9). Deep within the fabric of our being is a longing for eternal truth. God has placed within every individual a hunger for God. When we approach people with this knowledge, we can engage them with confidence, knowing that whether they realize it or not, their soul is hungry for God.

Understanding that every human being has a soul hunger for God, Jesus had no problem believing in people. He was not discouraged by those who seemed least interested in His message. He approached a Samaritan woman, a Jewish scribe, a Roman soldier, a Canaanite seeker, and a woman of ill repute. In each instance, Jesus looked for the best. He presented the truth but always in love. The foundation of His message was acceptance, forgiveness, grace, and the hope of a new life. He never minimized the value of truth, but He always presented truth in redemptive ways. Ellen White paints a beautiful portrait of Jesus' interaction with people: "Jesus did not suppress one word of truth, but He uttered it always in love. He exercised the greatest tact and thoughtful, kind attention in His relationship with the people. He was never rude, never needlessly spoke a severe word, never gave needless pain to a sensitive soul. He did not censure human weakness. He spoke the truth, but always in love."[1] The goal of this chapter is to discover how to apply Jesus' methods in our daily witness.

Discovering Jesus' method of dealing with people

We have discussed the Samaritan woman at the well in a previous chapter. However, there is one additional aspect of Jesus' discussion with the woman that is crucial to our understanding of sharing our faith. In the story, Jesus and the woman fall into conversation, and she eventually tests Him with the subject of an ongoing feud between the Jews and the Samaritans: "Sir, I perceive that you are a prophet. Our fathers worshiped on this mountain, and you Jews say that in Jerusalem is the place that one ought to worship" (John 4:19, 20). The proper place of worship was a divisive issue between their respective peoples. Jews and Samaritans did not get along, and the controversy had to do with the worship of God. Mount Gerizim, the Samaritan place of worship, became the main point of divergence between them, prompting a Jewish sage to raise and answer the question, "At what point can the Samaritans be accepted into Judaism? When they reject their belief in Mount Gerizim."

Here is the background of this debate. The Samaritans wanted to participate with the Jews in building the temple at Jerusalem, but because of their intermarriage with the nations around them, the Jewish leaders would not allow them to participate in building the temple. Consequently, they decided to build their own temple on Mount Gerizim.

Jesus could have easily entered into a theological debate with this woman over authentic worship, but He looked beyond her intellectual question and met her heart need. Her great need was not to have her religious questions answered. Her need was to find the acceptance, forgiveness, and new life that only Jesus could give. As a result of this one woman's conversion, all of Samaria was impacted. Jesus remained two days in this apparently unreachable place with these apparently unreachable people. The results were remarkable. John's Gospel declares, "Many of the Samaritans believed on Him because of the word of the woman who testified." Then John adds, "Many more believed because of His [Christ's] own word" (verses 39, 41). The conversion of the many Samaritans was only the beginning of a spiritual harvest in what seemed to be a barren land. Samaria was ripe for the gospel, and a few years later, it responded to Philip's preaching, receiving "the Word of God" (Acts 8:14).

What if Jesus had argued with the Samaritan woman? Suppose they had spent their time in a heated debate over where to worship? Most likely, it would not have gone well. Fortunately, Jesus looked beyond her comments to her needs. Successful witnesses for Christ have a winsome disposition and a winning attitude. They see the best in others.

Consider Christ's interaction with the Canaanite woman. The Canaanites were an idolatrous people who venerated the dead through their household gods. They also worshiped the pagan deities Baal, El, Asherah, and Astarte. These fertility cults were usually gods and goddesses of vegetation and the harvest. The heathens gave grain and fruit offerings to win their favor.

Many scholars believe that the Canaanites' religious rites also included human sacrifices, especially child sacrifice. If a Jew considered anyone an outcast, untouchable, and unwinnable, it would have been a Canaanite woman. Given this prejudice, Jesus' approach to this woman is masterful and unconventional.

In His divine wisdom, guided by the Holy Spirit, He reaches her in a way that seems contrary to His nature. She appeals for His mercy upon her and her daughter, pleading with Him to deliver the girl from demon possession (Matthew 15:22). Jesus responds to this heartfelt appeal with silence. He seems to ignore her, and His disciples plead with Him to send her away, yet she persists, prompting Jesus to make this astonishing statement: "I was not sent except to the lost sheep of the house of Israel" (verse 24). Jesus' dismissal of her request seems like discrimination. It appears He has come only for a select few.

Amazingly, the desperate woman does not take no for an answer. She appeals, "Lord, help me!" (verse 25).

Jesus now appears to reject her totally, saying, "It is not good to take the children's bread and throw it to the little dogs" (verse 26).

Undaunted by Jesus' rebuff, she tenaciously counters with a final appeal: "Even the little dogs eat the crumbs which fall from their master's table" (verse 27).

In this exchange with the Canaanite woman, Jesus' responses were born of a divine strategy. He was continually drawing her to deeper faith and revealing to His disciples the need to see the depth of faith in someone they would have turned away. In the end, Christ clearly said to the woman, in the presence of the disciples, " 'O woman, great is your faith! Let it be to you as you desire.' And her daughter was healed from that very hour" (verse 28). Remarkably, Jesus saw what others did not see. He saw "great faith" in this Canaanite woman.

Effective witnesses for Christ see the dawning of faith in the hearts of people in unexpected places. God often surprises us. He is working in ways and places we would not expect. If we have eyes to see, ears to hear, and minds to understand, we will sense the Holy Spirit's working in the lives of people all around us. The scales will fall from our eyes, and we will see others through Jesus' eyes. Christ saw people, not as they were but as they might become, refined and ennobled by His grace. He believed in them, so they rose to meet His expectations.

Jesus agreed with people where He could, accepted them where they were, and affirmed them when He was able. He developed caring relationships with people, and it was in the context of these relationships that He planted the seeds of faith and shared divine truth. As Ellen White so aptly puts it, "The gospel invitation is not to be narrowed down and presented only to a select few, who, we suppose, will do us honor if they accept it. The message is to be given to all. When God blesses His children, it is not alone for their own sake, but for the world's sake. As He bestows His gifts on us, it is that we may multiply them by imparting."[2] For Jesus, the field was the world, and every person in it was a potential candidate for the kingdom of God. He purchased each individual with His blood, and that is the good news we are called to share. Our appeal to the people of this world is to accept the salvation that Christ so freely offers.

The gospel: The basis of all acceptance

The foundation of all acceptance is the gospel. Christ has accepted us so that we can accept others. We can forgive others because Christ has forgiven us. We can have mercy on others because Christ has had mercy on us. Christ sees the best in us so that we can see the best in others. Jesus saw the thief on the cross, not as a young rebel but as a good boy who made some poor choices. He saw Mary Magdalene as a young woman seeking a divine love that would fill her heart with peace and joy. Jesus saw the Roman centurion, not as a ruthless, bloodthirsty member of the opposition but rather as one looking for a true Leader who could provide much more than Rome could offer. Jesus looked at the outcast, the defiled, the immoral, the thief, the drunkard, and the wealthy aristocrats all through Heaven's eyes. Jesus saw fertile ground where others saw only barren ground. Jesus saw possibilities where others saw only

83

problems. Jesus saw what the Holy Spirit could do when others saw only what sinful individuals had done.

The apostle Paul states it this way: "Therefore receive one another, just as Christ also received us, to the glory of God" (Romans 15:7). The apostle also stated, "And be kind to one another, tenderhearted, forgiving one another, even as God in Christ forgave you" (Ephesians 4:32). The law of kindness wins hearts; tenderheartedness, acceptance, and forgiveness open minds to the gospel. Treating others as Christ has treated us makes all the difference in our witness.

Some time ago, a poverty-stricken woman wandered down the street on a cold winter night. When she passed the Seventh-day Adventist church, she noticed the lights were on. She anxiously entered the fellowship hall, not having any idea what to expect. Life had been extremely hard for her. She had recently been through several traumatic experiences.

A healthy cooking class was in progress. She found a seat in the back of the room and sat with a woolen cap pulled down over her head, bundled in a winter coat. She was an oddity alongside the more sophisticated women attending the class that night. Fortunately, some of the women reached out to her. They made her feel welcome. They seemed to overlook her poverty and value her personhood. They overlooked the fact that she rummaged through the trash can looking for food when the class was over. They said little but tried to supply some of her needs.

She continued attending the class, and friendships developed. She began to bond with some of the women, and as the weeks passed, impressed by the kindness, love, and acceptance she experienced, she began to attend church each week and followed through with Bible studies.

Beneath the veneer, there was an intelligent and talented woman. As a child, she had taken piano lessons and was an accomplished pianist. Within two years, she was an active member of the church and one of its pianists. Seeing people not for what they are but for what they might become makes all the difference. Jesus had a winning attitude, and so can we.

Friendship opens the door to hearts, but it does not usually win people to Christ without our intentional witness. Positive relationships create confidence, but in and of themselves, they do not win people if they are not Christ-centered relationships. Jesus is "the way, the truth, and the life" (John 14:6), and He calls us to "speak the truth in love" (Ephesians 4:15).

A few practical suggestions

Think about the scenarios below. How would you deal with each case? Looking through the eyes of Christ, what do you see?

Scenario 1. A homeless man camps out in your church parking lot. He has been there for three nights. What are the appropriate ways to relate to him? Inappropriate ways? How can you be redemptive without turning the parking lot into a tent city for the homeless and negatively impacting the neighborhood?

Scenario 2. A Catholic business associate has just lost a wife due to an extended bout with breast cancer. He is troubled by the thought that she may be suffering in purgatory. How can you present the truth about the state of the dead in a comforting way without offending him?

Scenario 3. A young couple you know are not Seventh-day Adventists, and they have just lost a twelve-year-old son in a car accident. How can you provide the hope of Christ's return without trivializing the death of their son?

Based on this study of Christ's approach to people, here are a few ways to develop a winning attitude for souls:

1. Ask Jesus to impress you that all people have spiritual longings and are winnable to Christ.

2. Seek to develop positive, Christ-centered relationships with those in your sphere of influence.
3. Pray for opportunities to share divine truth.
4. Present biblical truths in the context of loving relationships.

Christ's call is for all believers

Witnessing is not an event for a few evangelistic superstars. Christ's call is for all believers. He invites us to participate with Him in the most exciting and fulfilling work in the world. Ellen White clearly states,

> All may find something to do. None need feel that there is no place where they can labor for Christ. The Saviour identifies Himself with every child of humanity. That we might become members of the heavenly family, He became a member of the earthly family. He is the Son of man, and thus a brother to every son and daughter of Adam. His followers are not to feel themselves detached from the perishing world around them. They are a part of the great web of humanity, and heaven looks upon them as brothers to sinners as well as to saints.
>
> Millions upon millions of human beings, in sickness and ignorance and sin, have never so much as heard of Christ's love for them. Were our condition and theirs to be reversed, what would we desire them to do for us? All this, so far as lies in our power, we are to do for them.[3]

God not only calls us but also equips and gifts us for service. He creates providential opportunities for us to share His love with others. Writing to the Corinthians, the apostle Paul mentions that God miraculously opened the way for him to proclaim the gospel on the European continent: "Furthermore, when I came to Troas to preach Christ's gospel, and a door was opened for me by the Lord" (2 Corinthians 2:12). The apostle recognized that the Holy Spirit did a work that he could never do. Only the Spirit can create receptivity in the minds of people. Only the Holy Spirit can open hearts to receive the gospel, and only the Holy Spirit can set men and women free from their prejudices, preconceived notions, and false ideas. Day by day, as we commit ourselves to participate with Jesus in reaching lost people, we will discover doors of opportunity opened by the Lord.

Daily request

Why not pray this simple prayer each morning? "Dear Lord, today I consecrate myself to You. Use me in Your service. Bring into my life someone with whom I can share Your love. Help me not to be so preoccupied with myself and my concerns that I miss seeing the opportunities to share Your truth with others. Lord, I am willing. Lord, I am available. I am your Servant. Use me in Your mission to lead someone to You. Amen." If you pray this simple prayer, God will powerfully use you in the most thrilling adventure of your life.

---

1. Ellen G. White, *Steps to Christ* (Nampa, ID: Pacific Press®, 1999), 12.

2. Ellen G. White, *Ministry of Healing* (Mountain View, CA: Pacific Press®, 1942), 102.

3. White, *Ministry of Healing*, 104.

Ten

An Exciting Way to Get Involved

I believe in small-group ministry because small groups are transformational. Thousands of church members around the world are actively involved in small groups, and they are experiencing their life-changing power. Small groups increase member involvement. They provide a safe place for the unchurched to share their concerns, allowing them to grow in their faith through prayer, Bible study, and discussion.   ↷

Small groups are not a new concept. They are as old as the book of Genesis and have been conducted throughout the centuries. Clarence Gruesbeck, writing in the April 1982 issue of *Ministry* magazine, shares the stories of three people powerfully impacted by their involvement in small Bible study groups:

↷

> Listen carefully to what three formerly unchurched people have to say about the effect on their lives, through the Holy Spirit, of small Bible study groups. "When my wife suggested that I attend her Bible study group, I was not interested. But I went because I had seen an incredible change in her. I'm glad I did, for I found something that was missing in my life. I have accepted Jesus Christ as my Saviour and Lord, and I am preparing for baptism."
>
> Another says, "What appealed to me at the Bible

study group was the realization that here were people who were experiencing a real relationship with Jesus Christ. God was working in their lives; that is why they accepted me when I was so unlovable."

And another, "I was impressed with the way members of the group helped one another. It was obvious that these people were filled with genuine love. You don't see much of that anymore, and I wanted that love in my life. I have discovered that it is very satisfying and rewarding."[1]

Small groups as the basis of nurture and outreach

In some parts of the world, small groups form the basis of spiritual nurture and outreach for the church. In other parts of the world, there are few small groups present in local congregations. Historically, small groups have always been central to spiritual growth and trace their roots to the time of Moses. In Exodus, they were part of Moses' organizational plan for Israel, and in the New Testament, they functioned in the ministry of Jesus and the first-century church.

Small groups serve multiple functions in the Bible. Some are nurture groups that emphasize prayer and Bible study. Other groups are focused on witness and outreach. Still others provide for Christian fellowship and the opportunity to share common problems. The most characteristic feature in Scripture is that small groups blend prayer, Bible study, fellowship, and witness. Successful small groups include all four of these elements.

Small groups without a mission focus do not survive long. Small groups with only a mission focus and little or no prayer, Bible study, and fellowship often "burn out" their members in ceaseless activity.

A biblical theology of small groups

In this chapter, we will take a brief look at Old Testament small groups but spend most of our time surveying Jesus' small-group ministry and the dynamic small-group ministry in the book of Acts.

The first verse in the Bible uses the plural word for God: "In the beginning God created the heavens and the earth" (Genesis 1:1). The word translated "God" is the Hebrew noun *Elohim.* Throughout Christian history, scholars have seen in this verse the concept of the Godhead: Father, Son, and Holy Spirit.

The idea of the Godhead is even clearer in Genesis 1:26. "Then God said, 'Let Us make man in Our image according to Our likeness.' " Here the plural name for God (*Elohim*) is combined with the plural pronouns "Us" and "Our" to once again indicate the plurality of the Godhead. Genesis chapter 1, combined with the further revelation of Scripture, provides rock-solid evidence that the Father, Son, and Holy Spirit are three separate eternal beings, existing in a small group of indivisible oneness and working together in varying roles to create the world and the cosmos (see Genesis 1:1, 2; Ephesians 3:9; Hebrews 1:1–3; Colossians 1:13–17).

The Bible teaches that God did not exist alone. The Father, Son, and Holy Spirit existed together from all eternity in intimate fellowship, abounding with love for one another. The love reflected in the relationship of the members of the Godhead and Their cooperation in Creation and Redemption is an example for small groups today.

We see this modeled in the New Testament, especially in the ministry of Jesus and His disciples. Luke 6:12, 13 records Jesus selecting the twelve disciples from among His followers. Before His selection, He "continued all night in prayer." As the Holy Spirit impressed Him, He chose twelve men to become part of His small group. Within that small group, His inner circle of Peter, James, and John were closest to Him. Jesus prayed with and for His disciples. He shared the Word of God with them. They ate together, shared one another's lives, and participated in Christ's mission.

Although they were men of varied backgrounds, personalities, and temperaments, Jesus was able to bring them together after His resurrection and infuse them with the single-minded focus of reaching the world with the gospel. Together, they were spiritually stronger than if they were alone. In unity, there is strength, and in division, there is weakness. When church members are organized into small groups and become united in mission, they become a powerful witness to the world.

Consider some examples of small-group ministry in the book of Acts. Acts 2 records that three thousand people were baptized on the Day of Pentecost. How were these early Christians nurtured? What kept the Christian church healthy? The record states, "And they continued steadfastly in the apostles' doctrine and fellowship, in the breaking of bread, and in prayers" (verse 42).

Note that these new converts were nurtured in small groups through prayer, social fellowship, and Bible study. Their lives were filled with "gladness" and "praise." The community was moved by the testimony of their words and the witness of their lives. This witness was so powerful that the "Lord added to the church daily" (verse 47). A united church organized for service is a powerful witness in the community.

In Acts 6, a problem arose within the church regarding the feeding of a group of widows. There was a "murmuring" that the Greek widows were being neglected in the daily distribution of food. This issue had the potential of dividing the church.

How was the problem solved? A small group of men, called deacons, was established to meet the need of the widows and seek the good of the body of Christ. They were instructed to come up with a solution. As a result, the unified efforts of these gifted men solved the problem.

In Acts 12, Herod imprisoned Peter, sealing his doom. The church formed a small prayer group in a home, members earnestly sought God, and Peter was delivered. A small group of committed praying believers made an eternal difference.

In Acts 16, the apostle Paul organized a gospel-medical missionary team to evangelize Greece. This team included Dr. Luke and some of Paul's young protégés. Churches established in Philippi, Thessalonica, and Corinth testify to the effectiveness of their work.

The above examples show that the New Testament small groups were quite varied. The Acts 6 group worked primarily within the church. The group in Acts 12 was a prayer group. And in Acts 16, the group was focused on evangelism.

This pattern suggests that we must be cautious not to make every small group the same. In the New Testament, small groups met different needs and performed various ministries, all for the good of the whole church.

Each group was involved in prayer, fellowship, service, and Bible study, but the ministry of the groups varied, based on the gifts of the members. Some groups were predominantly caring groups that ministered within the body of Christ, while other groups were mainly mission groups, focused on winning lost people to Christ.

The body of Christ

In 1 Corinthians 12, the apostle Paul uses the imagery of the body of Christ to describe the organizational structure of the church. Each member is essential to the function of the body. When we think of the human body, we recognize that the different members, or parts of the body, are organized into systems. These systems do not function independently. The human body is made up of eleven systems vital to the effective functioning of the entire body. A few examples are the digestive system, the circulatory system, the nervous system, and the respiratory system.

Imagine the respiratory system as a small group with different members providing oxygen to the cells. The group would be composed of the nose, mouth, larynx, trachea, bronchi, and lungs. The respiratory system brings life to the entire body through its air passages. Can you begin to understand why the Holy Spirit impressed the apostle Paul to use the body as an illustration of the church?

He states, "Now you are the body of Christ, and members individually" (verse 27). Members organized into small groups, each contributing their gifts to the whole, create a healthy environment for members' spiritual growth. The natural result of their growth is the positive witness of the church in the community.

When you think of the human body, every member has a function. There are no idle spectators. Each member of the body has a role to play. Verses 20–22 makes this point clear. "But now indeed there are many members, yet one body. And the eye cannot say to the hand, 'I have no need of you'; nor again the head to the feet, 'I have no need of you.' No, much rather, those members of the body which seem weaker are necessary."

Every member of the church is vitally important. Each one has been gifted for service within the body. Small groups become the vehicle God uses to focus the witness of each member for the good of the entire body. These interrelated groups, with varying roles and responsibilities, provide the foundation of a healthy church. Involvement in a small group fosters Christian commitment, trust, and accountability. Christianity is not a solo act. We are Christians in community, contributing to the cause by using our gifts in and for the community. God has placed the right gift mix in your church to accomplish His mission in your community.

Blended gifts

In addition to our personal witness for Christ, small groups provide an opportunity for the blended gifts of each member to be used to their maximum capacity. Everyone is not called to do the same thing, but we are called to use the gifts God has given us. Small groups are an exciting way to get involved. Here are a few small groups to consider.

> 1. *Sabbath School action units.* Adult Sabbath School classes can easily become effective small groups. They are already organized, and the next step is to plan a meeting one night a week to pray, fellowship, share a meal, study the Bible, and plan for outreach activities. In some parts of the world, these Sabbath School action units are the foundation of church growth.

> 2. *Ministry groups.* Ministry groups focus on outreach. They are mission-driven. Small groups of six to twelve

church members with similar gifts and interests unite to accomplish a specific ministry task. For example, a health-ministry outreach might include cooking schools, stress management seminars, or lifestyle seminars. Other examples might be family life ministry, youth ministry, and Bible-study ministry. In each of these ministries, the Holy Spirit leads members with similar interests to form a small group and use their gifts to reach out to the community.

3. Nurture groups. Small nurture groups of six to twelve people focus on caring for and strengthening the faith of existing church members. They often meet in homes for a three- to six-month period to share one another's joys, sorrows, struggles, and triumphs.

4. Mission groups. Mission groups consist of six to twelve people who regularly meet together to pray, study God's Word, fellowship, and grow in Christ and an understanding of His Word. They differ from nurture groups in the sense that their focus is outward. Each member invites a nonmember to attend the group with them. These groups are mainly focused on nonbelievers. Once they grow to ten to twelve people, they divide and begin another group.

Small-group structure

Small groups usually meet for an hour to an hour and fifteen minutes. They are composed of the following elements:

1. A sharing time. During the sharing time, the group leader invites members to share how their week has gone. He/she might ask whether anyone has a praise to share. Are there challenges that someone has faced this week? Does someone have a personal prayer request?

2. Prayer time. This is a time to open hearts to each

other and God, asking Him to meet our needs and thanking Him for the way He is guiding our lives. Members of the group bond in sacred fellowship as they pray for and with one another.

3. Study time. Small-group Bible studies are usually interactive, exploring a specific topic or studying a book of the Bible. Creating an atmosphere in which each participant feels comfortable in sharing thoughts is vital in the small-group setting. Typically, the studies last for about twelve weeks. Small-group members commit to attending the group meetings each week unless some unforeseen circumstances arise.

4. Fellowship time. Spend time at the end of the Bible study getting to know one another more deeply in a casual setting. Serving fruit juice, herbal teas, or water can encourage good conversation.

5. Mission or outreach planning. Whatever type of group you choose to establish, mission focus is paramount. Without an emphasis on outreach, the group can quickly become self-absorbed. Groups without a purpose can easily become problem-centered. Groups with a mission focus tend to thrive where groups that have an inward emphasis tend to die. Choose an outreach project and watch your group thrive.

Small-group leadership

In his helpful book on small-group leadership titled *8 Key Habits of Small Group Leaders*, David Earley outlines the effective habits of small-group leaders: "The eight habits can take a small-group leader, and those under him or her, to a new level. Whether an apprentice leader, a novice small group leader, a seasoned leader, a coach of small group leaders, a director of a district of groups, or a pastor of a large small group ministry, the eight habits will work. These habits lead to fruitfulness and multiplication. The eight habits will help leaders, and those under them, experience greater fulfillment in ministry."[2]

The eight habits of effective small-group leaders that Dave Earley describes are these:

1. Dream of leading a healthy, growing, multiplying group.
2. Pray for group members daily.
3. Invite new people to visit the group weekly.
4. Contact group members regularly.
5. Prepare for the group meeting.
6. Mentor an apprentice leader.
7. Plan group fellowship activities.
8. Be committed to personal growth.

If you believe God is calling you to lead a small group, review these small-group leadership characteristics, and ask for His direction.

John Wesley and small groups

John Wesley, the founder of Methodism, established small groups as the basis of his ministry and offered powerful insights on their value. The Methodist small-group principles have been effectively applied by secular educators and religious leaders ever since Wesley introduced them. Methodists were divided into classes of ten to twelve members. The class leader (assigned from among their ranks) had to meet each member of his class at least once a week. The leader was responsible for the spiritual care of the members of his group. They were "to inquire how their souls prosper; to advise, reprove, comfort, or exhort, as occasion may require; to receive what they were willing to give toward the relief of the poor."[3]

W. H. Fitchett wrote: "In Wesley's societies . . . a new and far-stretching brotherhood came into existence. It spread like a living net over England. It linked men and women, parted from each other by the widest differences of education and social position, of wealth and poverty, into a common household. . . .

The classes were a brotherhood; a brotherhood woven of spiritual ties, and so made indestructible."[4]

According to Albert Wollen, every major revival has been influenced by ready access to the Bible and the gathering of believers in small, intimate groups.[5] What happened in England during Wesley's time can happen in our society. Small groups are like family, bringing identity and fellowship to the lonely. The stranger is accepted regardless of his cultural, ethical, or religious background. Irrespective of his sin or his skin, he is loved, and that makes life worth living!

John Wesley was not the greatest preacher of his day, but his occasional friend and sometime nemesis George Whitefield was. He is said to have offered this lament: "My brother Wesley acted wisely," Whitefield said. "The souls that were awakened under his ministry he joined in class [small groups], and thus preserved the fruits of his labor. This I neglected, and my people are a *rope of sand*."[6]

Whitfield's point is thought-provoking. He is essentially saying that a casual Christianity that necessitates only listening to preaching, no matter how powerful that preaching is, can easily lead to a church full of spectators whose faith is like ropes of sand. If you desire to have a vibrant, growing Christian faith, get involved in a small group or, better yet, start one.

Here are three practical questions for you to prayerfully consider:

1. Have you ever thought of starting a small group in your home?
2. Is there a ministry group that the Holy Spirit has impressed you to join?
3. What would you think of your Sabbath School class becoming a Sabbath School action unit that meets once a month to pray, fellowship, study the Word, and plan a mission activity?

In the New Testament Christian church, there were no spectators. The same model works today. Get involved in a small group, and you will grow in Christ, in your relationships, and your witness to the world. ✍

1. Clarence Gruesbeck, "Small Group Evangelism," *Ministry*, April 1982, https://www.ministrymagazine.org/archive/1982/04/small-group-evangelism.

2. Dave Earley, *8 Habits of Effective Small Group Leaders: Transforming Your Ministry Outside the Meeting* (Houston, TX: Cell Group Resources, 2001), 15.

3. D. Michael Henderson, *John Wesley's Class Meeting: A Model for Disciples* (Wilmore, KY: Rafiki Books, 2016), 79.

4. W. H. Fitchett, *Wesley and His Century: A Study in Spiritual Forces* (London: Smith, Elder, and Co., 1906), 224.

5. Albert J. Wollen, *Miracles Happen in Group Bible Study* (Glendale, CA: Gospel Light, 1976), 32.

6. Holland M. McTyeire, *History of Methodism* (Nashville: Publishing house of the M. E. Church, South, 1904), 204, quoted in Henderson, *John Wesley's Class Meeting*, 30.

Eleven

Sharing the Story of Jesus

One of the greatest missionaries of the nineteenth century was Adoniram Judson. He and his wife spent most of their lives in Burma, where he mastered the language and translated the Bible into Burmese. He trained pastors, planted churches, entered new territories, and conducted evangelistic meetings. His life was consumed with sharing the Christ he loved with the Burmese people. At one point, he was imprisoned and tortured for his faith. His wife's witness and courageous defense of the truth during his imprisonment is legendary.

On one occasion, the local newspaper wrote a favorable article about him, likening him to a biblical apostle. When his wife told him about the report, he replied, "I do not want to be like a Paul or any mere man. I want to be like Christ. I want to follow Him only, copy His teachings, drink in His Spirit, and place my feet in His footprints. Oh, to be more like Christ!"[1] The power of evangelism is the power of the living Christ working through the living witness to change lives.

The power of New Testament witnessing is the power of personal testimony. The first-century believers shared a Christ they knew from experience. The apostle Paul makes this point clear in his epistle to the Philippians: "But what things were gain to me, these I have counted loss for Christ. Yet indeed I also count all things loss for the excellence of the knowledge of Christ Jesus my Lord, for whom I have suffered the loss of all things, and count them as rubbish, that I might gain Christ" (Philippians 3:7, 8). Paul knew Christ personally, experientially. It was from this intimate relationship with Christ that his witness overflowed to change the world.

Make-believe Christians will never change the world. When Christ dwells in our hearts through the ministry of the Holy Spirit, our lives are changed. It is out of the context of a changed life that authentic witness flows.

Witnessing is a task if it is merely a duty or religious obligation. It is delightful if it comes from a heart overflowing with love for Christ, the Redeemer. When we are in love, we enjoy talking about the one we love. This is true of human love and undoubtedly true of divine love. The power of New Testament witnessing was precisely this—believers spontaneously shared a Christ they loved. Witnessing was not a legalistic requirement; it was the heart's response to Christ's sacrifice on the cross. Ellen White says,

> When the love of Christ is enshrined in the heart, like sweet fragrance it cannot be hidden. Its holy influence will be felt by all with whom we come in contact. The spirit of Christ in the heart is like a spring in the desert, flowing to refresh all and making those who are ready to perish, eager to drink of the water of life.
>
> Love to Jesus will be manifested in a desire to work as He worked for the blessing and uplifting of humanity. It will lead to love, tenderness, and sympathy toward all the creatures of our heavenly Father's care.[2]

In this chapter, we will rediscover the power a personal testimony has to influence others for Christ. The transformative power of our testimony is not in telling how bad we once were or how good we now are. It is about the Christ who came to this sin-cursed world on a redemptive mission of love to redeem us. We can testify with assurance, not because of who we are but because of who He is. Our assurance lies not in our righteous deeds but in His perfect righteousness. We are secure, not in our tainted good works but in His sinless life.

Grace: The basis of all witnessing

The foundation of our witness is simply this: Christ loved us before we loved Him. Through His life, death, and resurrection, He gives us what we do not deserve so that we can share the grace of God with others who are undeserving. It is this grace, this unmerited favor, that saves us. Salvation is a gift that comes to us through His sinless life, His atoning sacrifice, His glorious resurrection, and His ever-present ministry in the heavenly sanctuary on our behalf. One of the most powerful statements ever written on the plan of salvation is found in *The Desire of Ages*. It is simple, direct, and incredibly profound. "Christ was treated as we deserve, that we might be treated as He deserves. He was condemned for our sins, in which He had no share, that we might be justified by His righteousness, in which we had no share. He suffered the death which was ours, that we might receive the life which was His. 'With His stripes we are healed.' "[3]

Motivated by His love, charmed by His grace, and redeemed by His sacrifice, we are changed. In Christ, the stranglehold of sin is broken in our lives. As guilt-ridden sinners, we are delivered from both sin's condemnation and sin's bondage (Romans 8:1, 15). Grace frees us. It liberates us. It puts a new song in our hearts and a new joy in our lives. We are now sons and daughters of God, adopted into His family and heirs of His kingdom (verses 14–17).

Grace changes us

Grace changes us. James and John, sometimes known as the Sons of Thunder, were transformed by grace. A person does not earn the moniker *Son of Thunder* because the person is mild, passive, and laid back. No, James and John were dynamos who could be quick-tempered or impatient. They were competitive and sought a position in Christ's new kingdom. However,

Christ's sacrificial love changed them and their entire being. James was eventually martyred, and John, who lived well into his nineties, never tired of telling the story of the love that changed his life. One writer commented that "John wrote with his pen dipped in love."[4]

The apostle Paul experienced the same love and declared that "the love of Christ compels us" (2 Corinthians 5:14). In other words, Christ's love compels a believer to tell the story of salvation. Ellen White states it this way: "Love is a heavenly attribute. The natural heart cannot originate it. The heavenly plant only flourishes where Christ reigns supreme. Where love exists, there is power and truth in the life. Love does good, and nothing but good. Those who have love bear fruit unto holiness, and in the end everlasting life."[5]

In Ephesians 2, the apostle Paul describes the change that takes place when an individual accepts Christ. He declares that we "once walked according to the course of this world" (verse 2). We "conducted ourselves in the lusts of our flesh, fulfilling the desires of the flesh and of the mind, and were by nature children of wrath" (verse 3). The expression "children of wrath" means that we are sinners by nature and worthy only of God's wrath and judgment. The prophet Jeremiah declares that "the heart is deceitful above all things, and desperately wicked" (Jeremiah 17:9). Isaiah adds that even our so-called righteousness is as "filthy rags" (Isaiah 64:6). The reason our righteousness is described as filthy rags is that it comes from a sin-polluted heart. Without Christ, we are hopelessly lost and in bondage to our sinful nature.

Paul continues his discussion of the plan of salvation by declaring that "God, who is rich in mercy," has "made us alive together with Christ" and "raised us up together, and made us sit together in the heavenly places" (Ephesians 2:4–6). He has saved us by His grace and not because of our righteous deeds (verse 8). By His grace, He pardons us from the guilt of sin and delivers us from the grip of sin. By His grace, He saves us from the penalty of sin and delivers us from its power. Salvation by grace releases us from the condemnation of sin and the bondage or domination of sin. We who were once dead in trespasses and sins are now alive in Christ. The expression translated in verse 5 as "made alive," or "quickened" (KJV), means "rebirth." In Christ, it is as if we are born all over again with a new identity in Christ. With this new walk in Christ, we are "His workmanship, created in Christ Jesus for good works, which God prepared beforehand that we should walk in them" (verse 10). The Greek word translated "workmanship" is *poiema*, from whence comes our English word *poem*. When Christ re-creates us for the glory of His name, He transforms our lives into poetry through the power of the Holy Spirit.

Grace for all

Here is some incredibly good news. God's grace is available to more than a select few. The apostle Paul makes it plain that it is freely given to all. He states, "But now in Christ Jesus you who once were far off have been brought near by the blood of Christ. For He Himself is our peace, who has made both one, and has broken down the middle wall of separation" (verses 13, 14). The expression "the middle wall of separation" is a remarkable one. The Jews would allow no non-Jew to enter the Jewish temple. There was a stone barrier four and a half feet high with thirteen large stone slabs on which, in both Greek and Latin, were a warning to Gentiles, or foreigners, that if they proceeded beyond this outer temple enclosure, they did so at the risk of their lives. The Jewish historian Josephus states this warning clearly: "There was a partition made of stone. . . . Its construction was very elegant; upon it stood pillars, at equal distances from one another, declaring the law of purity, some in Greek and some in Roman letters, that 'no foreigner should go in the sanctuary.' "[6] Gentiles had no access to the presence of God in the Jewish sanctuary. Christ changed all of that. His grace provides direct access to the Father. All who by faith receive the salvation that He so freely offers will have entrance into His eternal kingdom.

The gospel is for all. Salvation is for all. Forgiveness, mercy, pardon, and grace are for all. The New Testament believers grasped the marvel of His grace, and they could not be silent. They understood the assurance of eternal life in Christ. They lived to tell the story of His abounding grace. As we grasp the significance of His grace, we, too, will live to tell His story.

Sharing Jesus

Telling the story of Jesus is telling the story of how His grace has worked in our lives. Witnessing is not a spiritual gift given to only a very few people; it is the role of every Christian. Sharing Jesus is merely telling what Christ has done for you. It is enthusing about the peace and purpose that have come into your life through Jesus Christ.

Pray for opportunities to tell those around you about the joy you have in following Jesus. Tell them how you grasped His promises by faith and found them to be true. Share answers to your prayers or Bible promises that are meaningful to you. You will be surprised at how well people respond to genuine faith.

In an earlier chapter, we mentioned the demoniac. Just imagine the power of his witness as he shared what Christ had done for him. Who could possibly argue with a testimony that was so real? Changed lives are the most potent testimony possible. Some will take issue with what you believe. They will debate your theology and question your logic. But few people will argue against the evidence of a changed life. As Ellen White so beautifully states, "The strongest argument in favor of the gospel is a loving and lovable Christian."[7] The critics were silent in the face of the fantastic changes in the demoniac's life. As Christ's love flows through your life, others will be moved to seek the Christ who has changed you and given you such peace and joy.

Several years ago I was conducting evangelistic meetings on the Solomon Islands in the aftermath of a terrible civil war. During the war villages were burned, homes destroyed and stores looted. Many were wounded or killed in the fighting. One of the ruthless killers on the islands was Mr. D. It seemed he took delight in terrorizing communities with his gang members. He found enjoyment in destroying entire villages. He prided himself on never losing fights. Yet there was something missing inside. There was an emptiness within. He longed for peace, freedom from guilt, and a purpose for living.

One night after he was beaten badly by a rival gang, he had a dream of the four horsemen of Revelation. He remembered his uncle, a Seventh-day Adventist, on one occasion discussed Revelation's prophecies with him. He sought out his uncle to explain the meaning of his dream. In a course of Bible studies the message of Jesus and His hopeful plan for the future changed Mr. D's life. He met Someone stronger than him, Someone who loved him more than he could ever imagine. In Christ, he found forgiveness, grace, mercy, and a new power for living. His gang member friends were amazed. They noticed the change immediately. Soon most of the gang was attending our evangelistic meetings, and some of them accepted Christ and His last-day message of truth. The influence of this one man made a dramatic difference in the lives of those around him.

Stories like this can be repeated. When Christ changes a life, He uses that life to influence other lives for the kingdom of God. When we have the assurance of eternal life in Christ, we long to share the assurance we have found in Christ with others.

Christian assurance

How would you respond if someone asked you the question, Do you have eternal life? Would your answer be vague or specific? Would you say, "I sure hope so"; "I wish I knew"; or "I am not certain"? Jesus wants you to have the certainty of eternal life. The apostle John declares, "God has given us eternal life, and this life is in His Son" (1 John 5:11). He then adds words too clear to be misunderstood, "He who has the Son has life. . . . These things I have written to you who believe in the name of the Son of God, that you may know you have eternal life" (verses 11–13). As long as we have Jesus Christ living in our lives, the gift of eternal life is ours. He is life, and in Him, we have life. It is this assurance that gives power to our witness.

Some Adventist Christians are concerned about accepting the biblical teaching of the assurance of salvation because of Ellen White's statement indicating we should never say that we are saved.[8] A careful analysis of this statement reveals that she was speaking in the context of "once saved always saved." She was speaking of the false assurance of self-confidence, the idea that when I come to Christ, I can never fall away and be lost. This doctrine quickly leads to complacency in our Christian lives and justification of our sinful behavior. The grace of God is not "cheap." It changes our lives. Regarding the assurance of salvation in Jesus, Ellen White was clear: "Each one of you may know for yourself that you have a living Saviour, that he is your helper and your God. You need not stand where you say, 'I do not know whether I am saved.' Do you believe in Christ as your personal Saviour? If you do, then rejoice."[9]

Although Ellen G. White gave counsel and even strong warnings against false assurance, she wrote just the opposite to a woman who was a committed follower of Christ but who was experiencing depression in the face of a debilitating illness. She wrote these reassuring words to this suffering woman who was torturing herself in uncertainty and discouragement:

> The message from God to me for you is "Him that cometh unto me, I will in no wise cast out" (John 6:37). If you have nothing else to plead before God but this one promise from your Lord and Saviour, you have the assurance that you will never, never be turned away. It may seem to you that you are hanging upon a single promise, but appropriate that one promise, and it will open to you the whole treasure house of the riches of the grace of Christ. Cling to that promise and you are safe. "Him that cometh unto me I will in no wise cast out." Present this assurance to Jesus, and you are as safe as though inside the city of God.[10]

Clinging to the promises of God, we can live with confidence, sharing His love with all those we meet.

Life application

We can be effective witnesses for Christ because the assurance of salvation is ours in Christ. We can share Christ with others because He is our Friend, our Savior, and our Lord. We can tell others about living a joy-filled life in Christ because we know that the gift of eternal life is ours.

If we live in anxiety and uncertainty about our assurance of eternal life, our message to others is muted by our uncertainty. If you have any doubt about your assurance of salvation today, let His Holy Spirit lead you to sincere repentance, the conviction of sin, and confession. Claim Jesus' promises of forgiveness and acceptance. Walk into the future with the assurance that you are Christ's, and He is yours. Through Him, your witness will make a powerful impact on the world around you.

1. Source unknown, "To Be Like Christ," Bible.org, accessed November 4, 2019, https://bible.org/illustration/be-christ.

2. Ellen G. White, *Steps to Christ* (Nampa, ID: Pacific Press®, 1999), 77, 78.

3. Ellen G. White, *The Desire of Ages* (Mountain View, CA: Pacific Press®, 1940), 25.

4. Harold Penninger, *Walking With God* (Brushton, NY: Teach Services, 1996), 97.

5. Ellen G. White, "Because He First Loved Us," *Youth's Instructor*, January 13, 1898.

6. Josephus, *Wars*, 5.5.2, quoted in the *NIV Archaeological Study Bible* (Grand Rapids, MI: Zondervan, 2005), 1917.

7. Ellen G. White, *The Ministry of Healing* (Mountain View, CA: Pacific Press®, 1942), 470.

8. Ellen G. White, *Christ's Object Lessons* (Battle Creek, MI: Review and Herald®, 1900), 155.

9. Ellen G. White, "The Need of Missionary Effort," *General Conference Bulletin*, April 10, 1901.

10. Ellen G. White, *Manuscript Releases*, vol. 10 (Silver Spring, MD: Ellen G. White Estate, 1990), 175.

Twelve

A Message Worth Sharing

September 11, 2001, is forever etched in the hearts of Americans who woke up to the unspeakable tragedy of that day. They witnessed the World Trade Center crumble to the ground in a dreadful terrorist attack, killing more than three thousand people. But in the wake of that disaster, a remarkable and miraculous story of heroism emerged. It is the story of two survivors, as told in the book *Creature of the Word: The Jesus-Centered Church*:

A few of those who were buried beneath the rubble miraculously survived the toppling of the towers. Two of these individuals were Will Jimeno and John McLoughlin, a pair of Port Authority employees who responded to the attacks and were on the bottom floor when the south tower began to fall. They raced to an elevator shaft and amazingly survived the one-hundred-story collapse around them, but were buried dozens of feet down in the midst of an array of rubble. Trapped without water, breathing smoke-filled air, both Will and John had little hope of survival.

Yet as they lay there, pinned under a mountain of debris, something was stirring inside an accountant in

Connecticut they had never met.

Dave Karnes, who had spent twenty-three years active duty in the Marine Corps, was watching the scene play out on television just like the rest of us. But more than allowing it merely to trouble him, he decided to do something about it. He went to his boss and told him he wouldn't be back for a while.

Dave went to a barbershop, asked for a high-and-tight haircut, then stopped by his home to put on his military fatigues, hoping the uniform would allow him access into the blocked-off area surrounding Ground Zero. He drove to Manhattan at speeds of 120 miles an hour and arrived by late afternoon. While rescue workers were being called off the wreckage pile because of danger, Dave was able to stay because of the clout and credential that came with his military uniform. Finding another Marine nearby, the two men walked the pile together, seeking to save the lost.

After an hour of searching, they heard the faint sound of tapping pipes and yelling. Will and John had been trapped for nine hours by that time, completely incapable of working themselves free. Yet in the midst of all the rubble, a Marine who earlier in the morning had been working a spreadsheet in Connecticut found them. Of the twenty people pulled from the heaped-up remains of the World Trade Center, Will Jimeno and John McLoughlin were numbers eighteen and nineteen. And all because Dave Karnes took off his suit, put on rescue fatigues, and stepped into the despair and darkness of Ground Zero.

In the same way (but to an infinitely greater degree), God took off His royal robes, stepped into our dark and depraved culture, and served us. We were buried in the depths and rubble of our own foolishness with zero chance of pulling ourselves out of our own sin.[1]

In these pages, we have described the divine rescue Jesus has provided for us. Witnessing is the story of how He left the realms of glory and the majesty of heaven to redeem us. Witnessing is about the Christ who has plucked us from the rubble of this world and delivered us from certain death.

We have focused on Jesus as our example of self-sacrificial love in relating to people, revealing the character of God, and explaining the eternal truths of His kingdom. His witness was not only the witness of His words. It was the witness of His life. His actions revealed the truthfulness of His words. His life was a testimony that what He taught was true. As Jesus sacrificially ministered to those around Him, hearts were touched. The barriers of prejudice were broken down, and multitudes responded to His gospel appeals.

All effective witness flows from a heart that is filled with love for Christ and His Word. New Testament believers were passionate about their witness because they were passionate about Jesus. The truth about Jesus was present truth that burned in their hearts. In Christ, they saw the fulfillment of prophecies. In His life and teachings, they witnessed the glory of God. Describing the experience of the early church, the apostle Peter says that they were established in "present truth." *Present truth* is an expression that the apostle uses to define truth that is both relevant and urgent for that generation. Christ had come. There was nothing more important for these New Testament believers to proclaim than the Christ who was the fulfillment of prophecy. Jesus the Messiah was the consummation of the hopes and dreams of all faithful believers down through the ages. Through the life, death, and resurrection of Christ, salvation was available to all.

Jesus' last-day message

Just as God raised up John the Baptist to prepare the world for Christ's first coming, He has sent a special message to prepare the world for Jesus' second coming. In this chapter, we will study Jesus' final message to a dying world. We will discover His "present truth" message for an end-time generation preparing for His return. We will explore the message of His everlasting love, His abounding grace, and His eternal truth in the last book of the Bible. More specifically, we will study the three angels' messages of Revelation 14:6–12.

The book of Revelation is the revelation of Jesus Christ (Revelation 1:1). Each prophecy of the Bible's last book uncovers gems of truth about Jesus. This is especially true of Jesus' final message in Revelation 14. The first five verses of the chapter describe the redeemed people of God, far above the conflicts and trials of earth, living in heaven with Jesus forever. The last eight verses of the chapter describe the second coming of Christ and the earth's final harvest. The middle section, verses 6–12, is strategically placed between these two events. It contains God's end-time message to prepare all the inhabitants of the earth to be ready for the return of the Lord and eternal life with Him.

Revelation 14:6, 7 states, "Then I saw another angel flying in the midst of heaven, having the everlasting gospel to preach to those who dwell upon the earth—to every nation, tribe, tongue, and people—saying with a loud voice, 'Fear God and give glory to Him, for the hour of His judgment has come; and worship Him who made heaven and earth, the sea and springs of water.' "

Here is an urgent message. The angel flies in midheaven for all to see. It is eternal; the angel has the everlasting gospel. And it is universal; the message is to be proclaimed to every nation, tribe, tongue, and people.

The eternal gospel

The phrase "everlasting gospel" speaks of the past, the present, and the future. When God created humanity with the capacity to make moral choices, He anticipated that they would make errant choices. Once His creatures had the capacity to choose, they had the capacity to rebel against His loving nature. The plan of salvation was conceived in the mind of God before our first parents' rebellion in Eden (Revelation 13:8).

Ellen White says, "The plan for our redemption was not an afterthought, a plan formulated after the fall of Adam. It was a revelation of 'the mystery which hath been kept in silence through times eternal.' Romans 16:25, R.V. It was an unfolding of the principles that from eternal ages have been the foundation of God's throne."[2] The phrase "everlasting gospel" speaks of a God who loves the beings He has created so much that although He fully knew the consequences of their choices, He made provision for their eventual rebellion before they sinned. The gospel is the incredibly "good news" that Jesus will deliver us from sin's penalty and sin's power. By faith in His shed blood and His resurrection power, we are delivered from the guilt and grip of sin. As the apostle Paul says, "Sin must no longer rule in your mortal bodies" (Romans 6:12, GNT). Although at times in our humanness we may fail, we are no longer under the domain of sin. Its hold on us has been broken. Christ's plan to deliver us from the domain of sin was not an afterthought. God was not caught by surprise by the awful drama of sin.

There is another sense in which the gospel is everlasting. To a generation starved for genuine, authentic love and longing for meaningful relationships, the gospel speaks of acceptance, forgiveness, belonging, grace, and life-changing power. It speaks of a God who cares so deeply that He will go to any length to redeem His children. He wants them with Him forever.

Into all the world

According to the urgent, end-time message of the first of these three angels, the "everlasting gospel" is to be proclaimed to every nation, tribe, tongue, and people. Here is a mission so grand, so great, and so comprehensive that it is all-consuming. It demands our best efforts and requires our total commitment. It leads us from a preoccupation with our self-interest to a passion for Christ's service. It inspires us with something larger than ourselves and leads us out of the narrow confines of our earthly agenda to a grander vision.

There is nothing more inspiring, more fulfilling, or more rewarding than being part of a divine movement, providentially raised up by God to accomplish a task far greater than any human being could ever accomplish on their own. The commission given by God described in Revelation 14 is the greatest task ever committed to the church.

Fear God

The aged apostle John, a prisoner on Patmos, continues his urgent end-time appeal in Revelation 14:7: "Fear God and give glory to Him, for the hour of His judgment has come; and worship Him who made heaven and earth, the sea and springs of water." The Greek New Testament word translated "fear" in verse 7 is *phobeo*. The sense in which it is used here is not being afraid of God; it is the sense of reverence, awe, and respect. It conveys the thought of absolute loyalty to God and full surrender to His will. It is an attitude of mind that is God-centered rather than self-centered. The essence of the great controversy revolves around submission to God. Lucifer was self-centered. He refused to submit to any authority except his own. Rather than submit to the One upon the throne, Lucifer desired to rule from the throne.

The first angel's message calls us to make God the center of our lives. In an age of materialism and consumerism, when secular values have made self the center, heaven's appeal is to turn from the tyranny of self-centeredness to the peace of salvation and service.

Giving glory to God

Notice this contrast: Fearing God speaks of our attitudes. Giving glory to God speaks of our actions. Fearing God has to do with what we think. Giving glory to God has to do with what we do. Fearing God deals with the inner commitment to make God the center of our lives. Giving glory to God deals with how our inner convictions translate into a lifestyle that honors God in everything we do.

The apostle Paul explains what it means to give God glory in his urgent appeal to the church at Corinth. "Therefore, whether you eat or drink, or whatever you do, do all to the glory of God" (1 Corinthians 10:31). When our hearts are centered on God, our one desire is to give glory to Him in every aspect of our lives; diet, dress, and entertainment will reflect our commitment to God. We give glory to Him as we reveal His character of love to the world through lives committed to doing His will.

An end-time judgment

The passage continues, "Fear God and give glory to Him, for the hour of His judgment has come" (Revelation 14:7). The issues in the great controversy between good and evil will be finally settled. The universe will see that God is both merciful and just. He is both loving and righteous. He is both compassionate and fair. The judgment reveals that God has done everything He possibly can to save every human being. It reveals before a waiting world and a watching universe that God will go to any lengths to save us. There is nothing more that He could have done to redeem us. The judgment sweeps aside the curtain and reveals the cosmic drama in the great controversy between good and evil. It reveals God's character of self-sacrificing love in contrast to Satan's selfish ambition. In the judgment, all wrongs will be made right. Righteousness will triumph over evil. The powers of darkness will be defeated. Injustice will not have the last word; God will. All of life's unfairness will be gone forever.

Worship the Creator

Revelation 14:7 ends with an appeal to "worship the one who made heaven and earth, the sea and springs of water." This is a clarion call to worship the Creator at a time when most of the scientific world and the religious world have accepted the theory of Darwinian evolution.

Creation speaks of our value in God's sight. It speaks of our worth to Him. We are not alone in the universe, some speck of cosmic dust. He created and fashioned us. We did not evolve. We are not a genetic mutation. Creation is at the heart of all true worship, and the seventh-day Sabbath, as established at Creation, is the eternal sign of God's creative authority (Genesis

2:1–3; Exodus 20:8–11; Ezekiel 20:12, 20).

The Sabbath speaks of a Creator's care and a Redeemer's love. It reminds us that we are not cosmic orphans on this spinning globe of rock. It points us to a Creator who created us with a purpose and loved us too much to abandon us when we drifted from that purpose. The Sabbath reminds us of the One who has provided all the good things of life. Sabbath is an eternal symbol of our rest in Him.

True Sabbath rest is the rest of grace in the loving arms of the One who created us, the One who redeemed us, and the One who is coming again for us. It is the eternal link between the perfection of Eden in the past and the glory of the new heavens and the new earth in the future. The three angels' messages present the gospel in an end-time setting that meets the heart needs of a postmodern generation, desperate for belonging, identity, community, purpose, fairness, justice, and compassion.

Present truth makes a difference

All present truth is "present" because it makes a difference in our lives in the present. New Testament Christians who believed that the prophecies of the Old Testament testified to Christ as the Messiah were radically changed. They believed that the message of Christ's life, death, resurrection, and high-priestly ministry made an eternal difference. The reason they were so passionate about witnessing is that the message they shared made such a difference in their own lives. The three angels' messages are urgent, present truth for this generation. They reveal God's eternal truths to a world of religious confusion. They speak in trumpet tones of God's grace, obedience to His law, the eternal significance of the Sabbath, His soon return, and His final appeal to all humanity. In a generation seeking truth, looking for purpose, and striving for meaning, the message of Revelation 14 speaks with increasing relevance.

For many in this generation, truth is relative. There are no absolutes. There is no moral compass.

In the survey taken in early 1991, interviewees were asked, "Do you agree strongly, agree somewhat, disagree somewhat, or disagree strongly with the following statement: There is no such thing as absolute truth; different people can define truth in conflicting ways and still be correct." Only 28% of the respondents expressed strong belief in "absolute truth," and more surprisingly, only 23 percent of born-again or evangelical Christians accepted this idea! What a telling revelation! If more than 75 percent of the followers of Christ say nothing can be known for certain, does this indicate, as it seems, that they are not convinced that Jesus existed, that He is who He claimed to be, that His Word is authentic, that God created the heavens and earth, or that eternal life awaits the believer? That's what the findings appear to mean. If there is no absolute truth, then by definition nothing can be said to be absolutely true. To the majority, apparently, it's all relative. Nothing is certain. Might be. Might not be. Who knows for sure? Take your guess and hope for the best![3]

Seventh-day Adventists have been raised up by God in this last generation to proclaim the everlasting gospel in the glorious light of the messages outlined in Revelation 14. We have a prophetic destiny. We are not just another denomination among the many churches. We are a movement raised up by God to proclaim His final message to all humanity. We have an urgent end-time message to share, the message of our soon returning Lord. It is no accident that you were brought onto the stage of human history at this time. It is not happenstance that you have been led by God to understand the eternal truths of Revelation. As Scripture so aptly puts it, "To whom much is given, from him much will be required" (Luke 12:48).

You and I are called by God in this crisis hour of earth's history to be witnesses for Him. We are ambassadors of His grace and heralds of His truth. We have a much larger purpose for living than just marking time on this old earth. We are witnesses for the eternal Christ. Will you join me in committing your life to something much larger than yourself? Will you join me in sharing the good news of His last-day message with the world around you?

---

1. Eric Geiger, Matt Chandler, and Josh Patterson, *Creature of the Word: The Jesus-Centered Church* (Nashville, TN: B&H Publishing Group, 2012), 64, 65.

2. Ellen G. White, *The Desire of Ages* (Mountain View, CA: Pacific Press®, 1940), 22.

3. "Situational Ethics," Sermon Illustrations, James Dobson letter in 1991 quoting statistics from George Barna's *What Americans Believe*, accessed November 5, 2019, http://www.christianglobe.com/Illustrations/a-z/s/situational_ethics.htm.

Thirteen

A Step in Faith

An inspiring story of faith transpired during the reign of King Frederick William III of Prussia. Lynn Jost describes the king's predicament and the eventual resolution.

The recent wars had been costly, and in trying to build the nation, [the king] was seriously short of finances. He could not disappoint his people, and capitulating to the enemy was unthinkable. After careful reflection, he decided to ask the women of Prussia to bring their gold and silver jewelry to be melted down for their country. For each ornament received, he determined to exchange a decoration of bronze or iron as a symbol of his gratitude. Each decoration would be inscribed with the words, "I gave gold for iron, 1813."

The response was overwhelming. More importantly, these women prized their gifts from the king more highly than their former jewelry. The reason, of course, is clear. The decorations were proof that they had sacrificed for their king. Indeed, it became unfashionable to wear jewelry, and thus was established the Order of the Iron Cross. Members wore no ornaments except a cross of iron for all to see.[1]

A Step in Faith

We, too, as Christians, declare that no sacrifice is too great for the One who gave so much for us. We are motivated by His love to commit our entire lives to His service.

Genuine faith always leads to action. Members of the New Testament church were passionate about witnessing. Sharing Christ was the natural outgrowth of their relationship with Him. They were prepared to make the supreme sacrifice for His cause. Many of them suffered persecution, imprisonment, and even death. No sacrifice was too great for Jesus, who gave so much for them.

Their commitment to Christ often led them to take a leap of faith. Christ called them out of their comfort zones. The task before them was far too great for them to accomplish but not too great for God to accomplish. They grasped the promises of God and in faith went out to change the world.

The task before the church today is far beyond our capacity to accomplish. Christ is calling us to take a leap of faith. In this chapter, we will review the life-changing commitment of the New Testament church in the light of Christ's commitment to redeem us. Jesus was wholly surrendered to the Father's will. The single-minded focus of His life was the salvation of humanity. No sacrifice was too great to accomplish that goal.

Self-sacrificing love

Philippians 2:5–11 is one of the most magnificent passages in the entire Bible on the condescension of Christ. Some call this passage "The Song of Christ." The whole book of Philippians focuses on three major themes: rejoicing, humility, and faith. Chapter 2 highlights the theme of humility. Jesus left the magnificent glories of His exalted state in heaven, divested Himself of the privileges and prerogatives as God's equal, entered the realm of humanity as a servant, and died the lowliest of deaths on the cross. The apostle Paul uses this example of Jesus as a model for Christian living. Christ's sacrificial life of unselfish ministry is the model for all Christian faith. He left the celestial realms and came to earth as the "unwearied servant of man's necessity to minister to every need of humanity."[2] In the introduction to the book of Philippians, the *Andrews Study Bible* offers this additional insight: "Christians give up claims of equality and serve one another in love and humility to prevent the spirit of competition from flaring up. Through this act of self-lowering, Christians also distinguish themselves from the people of the world, who seek their rights and engage in struggles to achieve equality with their peers and superiors."[3]

A careful analysis of Philippians 2:5–11 reveals gems of truth for our lives today. The passage begins with these memorable words, "Let this mind be in you which was also in Christ Jesus" (verse 5). Earlier in the chapter, Paul presented the need for unity and unselfish humility. Now he focuses on Christ as our example of sacrificial living and ministry. The mind of Christ is the mind of service.

Jesus was committed to ministering to the needs of those around Him. Jesus was in the form (verse 5), or the very essence, of God. He possessed all the eternal characteristics and qualities of God. According to the *Seventh-day Adventist Bible Commentary*, "This places Christ on an equality with the Father, and sets Him far above every other power. Paul stresses this to portray more vividly the depths of Christ's voluntary humiliation."[4] Christ did not think it "robbery" to be "equal with God."

In other words, He recognized His eternal nature and His oneness with the Father but voluntarily left His position at the Father's side to "make Himself of no reputation." The literal translation of this phrase in verse 7 is He "emptied Himself." He divested Himself of all the kingdom glory. All the inherent characteristics and qualities that were His by His eternal nature and oneness with God were surrendered for our sake. He came, not in a kingly palace, the son of royalty, but as a humble, obedient servant. The Greek word for servant is *doulos*, meaning "bondservant" or "slave." Paul is contrasting two estates, the form of God and the form of a servant. Jesus went from the highest position to the lowest position, all for us. He surrendered His divine sovereignty for a life of sacrificial service. To have the mind of Christ is to have the mind of loving self-sacrifice for the salvation of others. The mind of Christ is one of ministry and service. It is one of mercy, compassion, forgiveness, and grace.

Christ's death on the cross reveals His heart of love. Genuine love always leads us to make sacrifices for the ones we love. Although feelings are associated with love, love is not a superficial, emotional feeling. Love is a commitment. It is a choice to seek the best for others. Love compels us to make sacrifices in our lives for the kingdom of God. It leads us to use the gifts He has given us, stepping out in faith to bless others.

The demands of love

After His crucifixion and resurrection, Jesus met a small group of His disciples on the shores of the Sea of Galilee. His goal in that early morning hour was to rebuild a man. Peter had recently denied Him three times, and Jesus hoped to evoke a response of love from Peter's heart, giving him a new sense of forgiveness, acceptance, and purpose. After a night of fishing in which these experienced fishermen did not catch a single fish, Jesus worked a divine miracle. Their nets were full to overflowing with a wonderful catch. Sitting around the campfire that morning in Galilee, Jesus asked Peter this pertinent question:

> "Simon, son of Jonah, do you love Me more than these?"
> He said to Him, "Yes, Lord; You know that I love You."
> He said to him, "Feed My lambs" (John 21:15).

In the original language of the text, there are two words for *love*. When Jesus asks Peter the question, He asks, "Do you love [*agape*] Me?" The word *agape* refers to love that flows from the heart of God. It is of divine origin. It is pure, unselfish love.

When Peter responds to Jesus, he does not use the word *agape*; he says, "Yes, Lord, You know that I love You." The Greek word Peter uses is *phileo*, a word that refers to a deep human bond; for example, the word *philadelphia* means "brotherly love." Jesus' response is to tell Peter to "feed My lambs." In other words, give your life in self-sacrificial service. Go to work for Me and minister to others. Jesus asks Peter the same question again in verse 16, using the same words, but the third time, in verse 17, Jesus changes the word for *love* when He asks the question. We do not see this in most languages, but it is apparent in the original language of the New Testament. Jesus no longer asks Peter, do you love Me with the divine *agape* love. He asks, Do you *phileo* Me? It seems as if Jesus is saying this, "Peter, I know that your love for Me flows through the weak channels of your humanity. You have denied Me three times, but I forgive you. My grace is yours. Begin where you are. Go to work for Me, and your love for Me will grow and expand into a deep divine love for others." Peter failed Jesus at a very critical moment in Christ's life, yet that did not disqualify Peter from serving. Jesus sent a forgiven, changed Peter to work for Him in the saving of souls.

As with Peter, our love for Christ will grow in service to others. The more we love Jesus, the more we desire to share that love with the people around us. The more we share His love with the people around us, the more our love for Jesus will grow. Ellen White shares this eternal truth in her classic volume *Steps to Christ*: "The spirit of unselfish labor for others gives depth, stability, and Christlike loveliness to the character, and brings peace and happiness to its possessor."[5] When we take a leap of faith and become actively involved in witnessing, we grow spiritually. Life's greatest joys come from sharing the love of God with others. As we daily seek opportunities to share what Christ means to us, we will see providential opportunities. The Holy Spirit will lead people who are seeking into our lives.

Many people fail to witness because they are unsure of what to say. Others are fearful of rejection or embarrassment. Witnessing is not out-arguing others. It is sharing what Christ has done for us. We make friends, then we make Christian friends, then we make Adventist Christian friends.

There is a beautiful statement by God's last-day messenger that assures us that our most powerful witness is our testimony.

"Our confession of His faithfulness is heaven's chosen agency for revealing Christ to the world. We are to acknowledge His grace as made known through the holy men of old; but that which will be most effectual is the testimony of our own experience. We are witnesses for God as we reveal in ourselves the working of a power that is divine."[6]

Adventist pioneers: Unusual sacrifice

In a collection of Adventist pioneer stories, the editors of the *Adventist Review* write, "There are incredible stories of faith and heroism demonstrated in the lives of our early Adventist pioneers. Many of our spiritual ancestors endured bitter cold, oppressive heat, rain, snow, poor-quality and scanty food, smoke-filled accommodations, and separation from family in order to take the gospel to far regions by boat, sleigh, train, buggy, and foot. How did a handful of mostly nonwealthy visionaries build churches and establish publishing houses, hospitals, and schools in the early days of our Adventist movement? The miracle stories of God's intervention coupled with the faith and sacrifice of His people abound."[7]

These early Adventists stepped out in faith, giving their all to share the good news of Christ's soon return. James and Ellen White were often in dire financial need in the early days of this movement. James imported commodities from the West to sell in the East to make a little income. On one occasion, he started a broom-making shop to earn extra money. He bought and sold animal hides. In a weakened condition, due to his debilitating sickness, he mowed a hayfield for a few dollars a day. The Whites used the few dollars they earned to survive and advance the cause of Christ.

As a single parent, John Nevins Andrews sailed to Europe with his two children in 1874 to advance the cause of Christ. Andrews was a brilliant scholar who knew seven languages fluently and could repeat the New Testament from memory. He worked tirelessly for the cause of Christ in Europe and died at the age of 54, having given his all for the Master.

Joseph Bates, the seasoned sea captain, accepted the Adventist message and became one of its ardent supporters. Captain Bates was one of the early promoters of the health message among Seventh-day Adventists. As a sea captain, he saw the harmful effects of alcohol and tobacco among his sailors and eventually banned all smoking and drinking on his ships.

He became interested in the Sabbath when he read a tract by T. M. Preble on the eternal nature of God's law and the Sabbath. After visiting with the Farnsworth family in Washington, New Hampshire, he became convinced that the Sabbath was given at Creation, commanded in the Ten Commandments, observed by the true followers of God in the Old and New Testaments, and kept by Jesus. (See Genesis 2:1–3; Exodus 20:8–11; Ezekiel 20:12; Luke 4:16; John 14:15.) Bates's commitment to Bible truth and his belief in the soon return of Christ based on William Miller's preaching motivated him to step out in faith, sell his home, and use the proceeds to advance the cause of Christ.

Abram La Rue: Motivated by mission

My point is not that we should go out and sell all that we have. God is not necessarily calling each one of us to do that right now, but He is calling us to step out in faith with the passionate desire to witness for Christ. We may find a model in Abram La Rue. This stalwart of faith applied to the General Conference to be sent as a missionary to China. The General Conference declined his request due to a lack of funds and La Rue's age. He was in his sixties at the time. Newly converted to the Adventist faith, he would not be deterred. He used his own funds and purchased passage on a vessel sailing to Hawaii. Once there, he sold Adventist literature on the island until he earned enough money to buy passage to China.

He arrived in Hong Kong on May 3, 1888. He was alone and had no Chinese contacts but began developing relationships and selling Adventist literature to the British sailors at the docks. Some of the sailors accepted the Adventist message and brought the Advent hope back to England. One report shared this experience about La Rue's faith and commitment:

Brother La Rue opened a mission on Arsenal Street, near the sea. "The large room was used for a gospel meeting hall, and a good stock of religious books and Bibles were attractively displayed. Among the soldiers and sailors and wayfarers the place soon became known as the headquarters for any man who needed a friend. The seed cast into the shifting sand of such a soil took root in some instances, and not a few men returned to their homes in the four quarters of the earth, thanking God for the beacon light set at this strategic point on the great highway of the Far East."[8]

Abram La Rue labored alone for fifteen years in China during the latter years of his life. Finally, in 1902, the newly arrived missionary, Pastor J. N. Anderson, baptized the first nine converts. At long last, La Rue saw the first fruits of his labors.

What was it that motivated him and other Adventist pioneers to travel to the ends of the earth to proclaim the soon coming of Jesus? What prompted them to leave their friends and relatives to go to sometimes-hostile lands? What led them to make such financial and personal sacrifices? Why did they step out in faith and give their all for the cause of Christ? There is just one reason: they were changed by the grace of Christ. The Adventist message changed their lives, and they were compelled to step out in faith to share God's love with others.

Christ's sacrifice motivates our action
David Livingstone once commented,

> People talk of the sacrifice I have made in spending so much of my life in Africa. Can that be called a sacrifice which is simply paid back as a small part of a great debt owing to our God, which we can never repay? Is that a sacrifice which brings its own blest reward in healthful activity, the consciousness of doing good, peace of mind, and a bright hope of a glorious destiny hereafter? It is emphatically no sacrifice. Say rather it is a privilege.

Anxiety, sickness, suffering, or danger, now and then, with a foregoing of the common conveniences of this life, may make us pause, and cause the spirit to waver, and the soul to sink; but let this only be for a moment. All these are nothing compared with the glory which shall hereafter be revealed in, and for, us. I never made a sacrifice. Of this we ought not to talk, when we remember the great sacrifice which He made who left His Father's throne on high to give Himself for us.[9]

David Livingstone clearly understood that whatever he sacrificed for the cause of Christ, Jesus' sacrifice for him was much greater.

As the apostle Paul passionately stated, "The love of Christ compels us" (2 Corinthians 5:14). In the light of Christ's love and His soon return, David Livingstone and the early Adventist believers were compelled to share the message of His love. They believed Christ's words, "And this gospel of the kingdom will be preached in all the world as a witness to all the nations, and then the end will come" (Matthew 24:14).

Considering the legacy of past faithful believers and standing in the blazing light of eternity before us, Jesus invites us to take a step in faith and commit all our lives to His service. His love compels us to give our all to His cause. Will you pause for a moment and commit your life to share His love and truth with the people in your sphere of influence? Will you dedicate your life to witness for Him in this crisis hour of earth's history? Why not bow your head and ask Jesus to place in your heart a burning passion to be an ambassador for Him?

---

1. Lynn Jost, "Sacrifice," Sermon Illustrations, http://www.sermonillustrations .com/a-z/s/sacrifice.htm.

2. Ellen G. White, *The Ministry of Healing* (Mountain View, CA: Pacific Press®, 1942), 17.

3. "The Epistle to the Philippians: Message," *Andrews Study Bible*, NKJV (Berrien Springs, MI: Andrews University Press, 2010), 1552.

4. Francis D. Nichol, *The Seventh-day Adventist Bible Commentary*, vol. 7 (Washington, DC: Review and Herald®, 1980), 154.

5. Ellen G. White, *Steps to Christ* (Nampa, ID: Pacific Press®, 1999), 80.

6. Ellen G. White, *The Desire of Ages* (Mountain View, CA: Pacific Press®, 1940), 347.

7. "Pioneer Stories," Adventist Heritage Ministries, accessed November 5, 2019, https://www.adventistheritage.org/ahm-sites/pioneer-stories.

8. Wu Chook Ying, "Abram La Rue," Adventism in China, 2011, http://www.adventisminchina.org/individual-name/expatriates/larue.

9. William Garden Blaikie, *The Personal Life of David Livingstone, Chiefly From His Unpublished Journals and Correspondence in the Possession of His Family* (London: John Murray, 1903), 190.